T0277529

MARCELO
BIELSA
vs THE PREMIER LEAGUE

MARCELO
BIELSA
VS THE PREMIER LEAGUE

LIVING, LOVING AND LOSING
BIELSABALL
FOREWORD BY BRYN LAW

ROCCO DEAN

First published by Pitch Publishing, 2023

Pitch Publishing
9 Donnington Park,
85 Birdham Road,
Chichester,
West Sussex,
PO20 7AJ
www.pitchpublishing.co.uk
info@pitchpublishing.co.uk

ISBN 978 1 80150 558 1

Typesetting and origination by Pitch Publishing
Printed and bound in India by Thomson Press

Contents

Foreword by Bryn Law 9
Introduction 13

Part One: 2020/21 – Marcelo's Masterpiece, From Behind Closed Doors

Pre-Season 2020/21 17
September 2020. 21
October 2020 30
November 2020. 41
December 2020. 55
January 2021 73
February 2021 83
March 2021. 96
April 2021 105
May 2021. 117
The Class of '21. 133
Premier League table 2020/21 135

Part Two: 2021/22 – The Return of the Fans, and the Curse of the Damned United

Pre-Season 2021/22 139
August 2021 143
September 2021. 152
October 2021 160
November 2021. 170
December 2021. 180
January 2022 191
February 2022 202
March 2022. 220
April 2022 233
May 2022 242
Premier League table 2021/22 263

Epilogue 264
First Impressions of Bielsaball 266
Bielsa Era Stats 269

This book is dedicated to Marcelo Bielsa, whose transformation of Leeds United inspired me to start writing for the first time as an adult, and to submit my work to a publisher.

Four days after posting him my account of his first season at Elland Road, Marcelo spontaneously turned up on my doorstep with presents of thanks. It was a moment to cherish for the rest of my life, something I will always feel blessed for, and it gave me the motivation and belief to turn my ramblings into a book worthy of publication. I could never have dreamed of being a published author before Marcelo came into my life, but five years on from his appointment I have written four books about Leeds United, with another on the way. Marcelo Bielsa didn't teach me to write but he dragged the potential out of me, so you can file me with Phillips, Cooper, Ayling and Dallas, and countless others around the world who have been touched by the divine influence of El Loco.

When I wrote to Marcelo requesting permission to use the story of his visit in *Marcelo Bielsa vs the Damned United*, he told me he valued the moment as much as I did. Instinctively, I took his comment with a pinch of salt, but perhaps he truly meant it, knowing he had still delivered happiness even through the bitter pain of missing out on promotion. He was loved in defeat, which must hold more value than being loved in victory.

'The repercussions of his art have infinite recognitions.' They are the words Marcelo spoke in tribute to Diego Maradona upon his death, words that ring true about The Great Man himself. Never has there been, nor will there ever be, a greater role model than El Loco.

Foreword by Bryn Law

AFTER 30 years covering Leeds United and 30 years living in this great city, the question I still get asked most by those who know what I do is, 'Are you a Leeds fan?' The answer to this is, in one sense, quite simple. I'm a Wrexham fan. I saw my first game in 1979 and I've been going to watch them ever since, when work allows. Work, of course, includes covering Leeds United.

I turned down the opportunity to do my first Leeds commentary in 1993 because I was off to The Racecourse to see if Wrexham could win the Third Division (today's League Two) title, on the same day Leeds finished their Premier League campaign at Coventry. That was a long time ago though and things have changed a little since. When Leeds went to London to play Brentford on the final day of season 2021/22, I travelled down on a train from Selby and there were Wrexham fans on the same platform, getting the same train, heading for Wembley and an FA Trophy Final appearance. I wasn't going to be among them. I had my own cup final to cover.

So, when people ask me, I'm most likely to say, 'Well, I'm a Wrexham fan but ... ', then launch into a wide-ranging explanation about how I've been in the city so long, have seen more Leeds games than those of any other club, have loads of friends who are Leeds fans, how much benefit the city derives from a successful club before finally conceding, '… so you could say I'm a supporter of Leeds.' Ultimately, it's a cop-out because, as any fan knows, you can't really declare allegiance to two clubs. It just doesn't work like that in our fan culture. It's like wearing a half-and-half scarf.

My first trip to Elland Road came in 1988. Adrian Chiles booked the minibus and rounded up a few uni mates to join him on his pilgrimage to see West Brom in the midst of a fine run of form, but the Baggies lost. Elland Road as viewed from the away terrace seemed a pretty scary place, but now it's a place that feels like home. That sense developed once I'd started covering the club in earnest, generally in the company of Norman Hunter, a wonderful and much-missed man from whom I learned so much, about life as well as football and Leeds United.

I threw myself into the commentaries with a fan's energy, trying to always remember my own experiences of travelling away in transit vans with mates, and to apply that experience to the way I described the games. I had Norman as the expert; I could be the fan with the mic.

The rapport we seemed to establish with the supporters drew me in. Emotionally I found I was investing more and more and, even after I'd moved on to Sky and found myself reporting almost daily on a spectacular rise and fall, it was impossible not to feel wrapped up in events at this crazy club. I felt the embarrassment of the slide down to League One. I was on duty at Elland Road on the day it happened; the stadium and the city stunned by this almost unthinkable occurrence.

The climb back was well under way when I returned to commentate on Leeds once more. I'd watched in disbelief as Leeds threw away that play-off lead against Derby County but then found myself back on the gantry for the first home game of the following season. What a season that proved to be. I thought I'd seen it all in a long career; I'd barely scratched the surface. Incredible football, lockdown, fans dancing on my car roof to celebrate promotion, and then commentating on the moment the trophy was lifted. It was an unforgettable season.

What followed makes for a terrific story as well, and I was delighted to be asked to contribute my own perspective. I count it as one of the greatest privileges of my career to be given the chance to be present at all Leeds's games on that return to the top flight. I was there when the fans couldn't be; I knew how fortunate that made me. Even more so given the quality of the football Leeds United played. Bielsaball was beautiful.

When the fans were finally allowed back in, the atmosphere inside Elland Road went beyond even those early years when I'd first been covering the club in the Premier League. The challenge for me and Tony Dorigo on commentary was often being able to actually hear each other, even through headphones. The joy at finally seeing Leeds back at this level barely wavered all season, even though results were not as good, and there were some truly unforgettable moments. In those moments and many others, the Premier League was reminded about what it had been missing in Leeds's long absence – a noisy, passionate capacity crowd crammed into a gloriously rickety old ground that's the antithesis of the big, shiny, boring modern-day stadia; this is a ground where every seat and step has a story to tell.

This is the story of Leeds United's return to the top level, and what a story it is.

Introduction

IN AUGUST 2001, Peter Ridsdale outlined plans to build a new home for Leeds United, with the intention of giving David O'Leary 'the world-class stadium his team deserved' by the start of the 2004/05 season. I said I'd rather be relegated than leave Elland Road, and the Football Gods answered my prayers. Within a year O'Leary had been sacked, within two years his team had been decimated, and within three years – the start of the 2004/05 season – Leeds had been relegated to the newly branded Coca-Cola Championship.

I am proud of my foresight at the tender age of 17. With Ridsdale as chairman a prosperous Leeds United would have led the way as football waved goodbye to its working-class heritage, and as much as I loved watching our brilliant young team sweep away nearly all comers, I loved our fans more than our players and I loved going to Elland Road most of all. As Leeds fell from grace, football for our rivals changed for ever. Anfield, Old Trafford and Stamford Bridge were flooded with tourists and day-trippers, keener to film goals than celebrate them. Highbury, White Hart Lane and Maine Road were consigned to the history books, replaced by high-tech, multipurpose arenas, designed to maximise corporate income. Goodison, St James' Park and Villa Park survived, but their famous atmospheres were a thing of the past, sterilised by the transformation of elite football from a sport into an international business.

My foresight, however, was sprinkled with naivety. I was 20 years old when Leeds were relegated at Bolton, but my disappointment was soon replaced by excitement for the adventure to come. I was excited about visiting lots of new grounds, excited about the signings of Michael Ricketts and Julian Joachim (deary me), and excited about celebrating promotion. It was inevitable that a club the size of Leeds United would regain their Premier League status, but I never thought I would be 36 years old by the time they did. Had I known we would go through 16 seasons, 15 managers, five owners and over 100 loan signings, perhaps I would have bulldozed Elland Road to the ground myself.

It was a long and painful road, but my wish feels vindicated. Leeds were returning to the big time with our famous stadium intact, the working class at their core and a messiah at the helm, who would surely be proud of me for putting the ultimate value on the human aspects of football.

Part One:

2020/21 – Marcelo's Masterpiece, From Behind Closed Doors

Pre-Season 2020/21

LEEDS WERE back in the big time, but preparing for life in the Premier League was only one aspect of a very strange pre-season. Six months had passed since Covid-19 robbed us of the freedom to attend matches, and although lockdown was over and the country was tentatively creeping back to normality, mass gatherings were still forbidden. The data would continue to be monitored (Covid cases, hospitalisations and deaths) and plans were afoot to allow limited numbers of fans to return, but the first month of the season, at a minimum, would be played behind closed doors and it was still unclear when the wait to watch Premier League football at Elland Road would end.

The pandemic had also played havoc with the football calendar, resulting in the shortest pre-season in history. Most clubs had six weeks between their final match of the 2019/20 season and the start of 2020/21, although the teams who had made it to the latter stages of the European competitions only had four weeks (the quarter-finals onwards were shoehorned into a two-week period in August). Leeds had the luxury of seven and a half weeks and spent most of it courting Ben White, the loanee centre-back who had shone in their promotion season. Parent club Brighton & Hove Albion refused to sell and with two weeks to go until the big kick-off there were still no new faces in the first-team squad, then on the last Saturday of August two arrived at once. In the morning the club smashed their 20-year-old transfer record with the £27m signing of Spanish international striker Rodrigo Moreno from Valencia, and in the evening another £13m was spent on German international defender Robin Koch. It had taken Leeds 14 years to amass a £40m spend in transfer fees following relegation from the Premier League, but ahead of their return they had matched that same outlay in 14 hours. Welcome to a whole new ball game.

The short turnaround was further complicated by an international 'break' in the week before the Premier League began. Coincidentally, the UEFA Nations League pitted the two new signings against each other, and if scouting Leeds players during a match between Germany and Spain wasn't strange enough, elsewhere the best young player in the world, Erling Haaland, made a beeline for Stuart Dallas after Norway hammered Northern Ireland 5-1. Dallas nearly jumped out of his skin when Haaland – born in Leeds and the son of former cult Whites hero Alfie – sang 'Marching On Together' in his ear, and asked for his shirt. However, the highlight of international week was undoubtedly Kalvin Phillips winning his first England cap. The Yorkshire Pirlo had never played a Premier League game, nor represented England in any age group, but there he was, with three lions on his chest and Christian Eriksen in his pocket. I was immensely proud of Phillips – such a lovely lad and a terrific player – and so too was Marcelo Bielsa, who gifted him a classic

Newell's Old Boys shirt to congratulate him on his call-up. Phillips returned the gesture by giving El Loco his debut England shirt as a thank you for everything he had done for his career, and they all lived happily ever after.

Another strange aspect of pre-season was having an out-of-contract manager throughout. Bielsa would only sign contracts from one year to the next, to protect the freedoms of the club and himself, but despite being out of contract he continued as normal, masterminding his assault on the Premier League from Costa Coffee in Wetherby, where he posed with fans for socially distanced selfies on a daily basis. He looked so happy and content too, as if the weight of the world had been lifted from his shoulders when he lifted the EFL Championship trophy back in July. Only on the eve of the season did El Loco finally put pen to paper on his one-year extension.

It was also strange not knowing what to expect or even hope for in the coming season. I could envisage Leeds taking the Premier League by storm and pushing for European qualification, but I had my concerns too. Even if top-flight teams couldn't handle the intense pressing and all-out attack of Bielsaball, I worried that our inefficiency in front of goal – such a frustration in the Championship – would be more regularly punished by higher-class opposition. I also worried that Leeds wouldn't be able to dominate possession like they could in the Championship, and as a result, wouldn't have the legs to press like maniacs for 90 minutes. Then there was the simple worry that some players might not cope with the step up. It was impossible to draw any conclusions from pre-season matches because there basically weren't any, and attempting to draw comparisons with the promoted clubs from 2019 only complicated things further. Championship champions Norwich had finished rock bottom, runners-up Sheffield Utd just missed out on a Europa League spot, and Aston Villa spent £100m just to survive by the skin of their teeth, and only thanks to malfunctioning goal-line technology.

Survival was the minimum requirement, but my ultimate dream was for El Loco to save football from the cesspit it had sunk into. Diving, feigning injury, wasting time, claiming for absolutely anything, complaining about absolutely everything; it had all become so common at the top of the game and was not only encouraged by managers but accepted by officials and even pundits. This blatant (and mostly needless) lack of sportsmanship had stopped me from watching top-level football – I couldn't go two minutes without being enraged by something and switching off in disgust – but Bielsa's team would not conform and I hoped his refreshing approach would resonate through the elite; that opponents would be embarrassed when facing a team playing with honour, that they would realise the gains from all the antics and theatrics are not worth the cost to the brand of football, not to mention their own personal and professional pride. The Loco Way was sure to gain a bucket-load of admiration, but his team would need to be successful for football to truly embrace The Great Man's philosophy.

September 2020

Bryn Law – 'I knew from experience that the Premier League was a very different league to the one Leeds United left behind. It had grown massively since Leeds were last in it and I felt it would be a shock to the system to come up against teams that have quality players throughout the squad. But Leeds didn't just face the challenge, they smashed it, playing fabulous football that was a joy to watch. There were so many great goals scored, so many great Leeds performances, and one or two teams were proper steamrollered. But the key to the season was blowing away the teams in their proximity and, home or away, pretty much every team was beaten.'

The Premier League
1st to 4th: Champions League qualification
5th to 7th: Europa League qualification
18th to 20th: Relegation to the Championship

Liverpool 4 Leeds United 3
Marcelo Bielsa finally had the platform he deserved, the most watched league in the world, and the fixture list provided an epic curtain-raiser – a trip to Anfield, to take on the reigning champions. As a pure football romantic, El Loco may have hand-picked this fixture despite it

being the toughest possible start; after all, it was a game he'd been preparing for since arriving at Elland Road. In one of his early press conferences Bielsa revealed, 'Before sleeping I imagine we are playing against Liverpool, and I always think we can beat them.' If we were to take his words literally he would have imagined beating Liverpool over 700 times, but with no fans in the ground this was not the match that Bielsa had dreamed about, a point he emphasised in his first Premier League media day: 'We are going to Anfield, but Anfield is only Anfield when it is full.'

Bielsa's opposite number, the exuberant Jürgen Klopp, was also a messiah in his adopted city. During El Loco's two-year odyssey in the Championship, Klopp had posted the second- and third-best points tallies in English football history, also winning the Champions League, the World Club Cup, the UEFA Super Cup and the Premier League, and his side were currently 59 games unbeaten in the league at home. This was a true managerial blockbuster, but there was a chasm the size of the Grand Canyon when comparing the value and achievements of each set of players, so it was hard to expect the Friday night Premier League opener to live up to its billing. The match didn't just live up to its billing, it broke new ground, introducing the Premier League to a type of football it had never seen before: Bielsaball, at its most exhilarating.

Leeds suffered a nightmare start, losing captain Liam Cooper to injury before kick-off, then losing parity when Robin Koch gave away a penalty for handball less than three minutes into his debut. It was a very harsh decision – the ball deflecting off Koch's knee on to his hand, with nothing he could do – so harsh that within a few days the handball rule was changed so that other clubs would not suffer such unjust punishment. That was no use to Leeds though, and when Mo Salah slammed the ball down the middle of the net I feared the worst.

United spent the next five minutes camped in their own half, but signs of life emerged when Hélder Costa had a goal disallowed for offside, then Patrick Bamford broke clean through but couldn't finish. The visitors had settled into the match and were growing in confidence, and on 12 minutes they equalised in spectacular style. Kalvin Phillips picked the ball up deep in his own half and showed the world why he was known as the Yorkshire Pirlo, by pinging a sumptuous pass for Jack Harrison to chase down the left wing. The Manchester City youngster was entering his third season on loan at Elland Road but we had never seen the likes of what he did next; it was as if he'd collected the invincibility star on *Super Mario*. Harrison plucked the ball out of the air with his right foot and jinked inside Trent Alexander-Arnold with his left, without the ball even touching the ground, then nutmegged Joe Gomez and rifled past Alisson from the edge of the box. I couldn't believe what I'd just seen. It was a dream goal for Harrison, and at the Kop end too (although I suppose the Kop is only the Kop when it is full).

For the rest of the first half it was non-stop, end-to-end football. Leeds attacked as relentlessly as they defended, throwing men forward at every opportunity and harrying their opponents all over the pitch. 'It gladdens the heart,' remarked legendary commentator Martin Tyler, while his co-commentator, Jamie Carragher, wondered whether he was watching a computer game, such was the ferocious pace and constant action. By half-time there had been five goals, another two disallowed, and an early contender for save of the season when Illan Meslier acrobatically rescued Pascal Struijk from an unfortunate own goal. Liverpool led 3-2 and everyone had the chance to catch their breath.

I was watching with a group of friends at Paddy's pad, and we were all amazed at how well the Whites had played. We'd known what they would try to do, but seeing it work against one of the best teams in Premier League history was thrilling. Soon after half-time we were celebrating deliriously again, as Leeds equalised for a third time through Mateusz Klich's brilliant flick and volley into the net. It was a goal to rival Harrison's – what a shame there were no Leeds fans in the Anfield Road end to witness it (the away end is definitely only an away end when it is full).

The pivotal moment of the match came in the 75th minute. With the teams locked at 3-3, Leeds won a free kick 30 yards from goal. The Yorkshire Pirlo stood over the ball, and the guests at Paddy's all rested their drinks on the floor, just in case. We began to celebrate as the ball glided over the wall and past the despairing dive of Alisson, but our celebrations were aborted as it curled inches past the post. This narrow escape seemed to jolt the champions into life, and after ten minutes of heavy pressure they won a penalty three minutes from time. Fans of symmetry must have been dancing in the streets, especially as it was Leeds's other big-money signing who gave this one away, and Rodrigo's 'striker's challenge' on Fabinho was punished by Salah, who completed his hat-trick to put Liverpool 4-3 ahead.

Leeds couldn't muster a fourth equaliser, and at the final whistle the camera panned straight to Jürgen Klopp who let out a sigh of relief and mouthed, 'Wow!' Like us, Klopp was not surprised by Leeds's approach, but he was clearly surprised by how hard it had been to overcome and enthused in his post-match interview, 'What a game, what an opponent, what a performance from both teams. I loved that, football at its best.'

After 16 years away from England's top table, the fact Leeds had gone toe-to-toe with the very best made me almost indifferent to the defeat. It had been a sensational return and I was bursting with pride as the pundits fawned over Leeds's performance, with Sky's Gary Neville describing it as 'a thing of beauty'. Also, I realised that in two years we had never really seen Bielsaball in all its glory. We had seen the pressing, the patterns of play and the aggression, but in the Championship it was never possible to see the fearless nature of El Loco's attacking philosophy. Effectively playing a front five at the home of the reigning world champions, in your first Premier League match – that is the true beauty of Bielsaball.

'I can never be happy in defeat.' El Loco's post-match comment was a paradox of his belief that bringing happiness to the public is the most important thing in football, but in defeat his obsessive brain won't have allowed him to register the possibility that the Leeds fans were, for once, happy losers.

Leeds United 4 Fulham 3

On a Championship fixture list Fulham at home always presented a daunting challenge, but in the Premier League this was a team Leeds would expect to put to the sword. The task was made a little easier with the return of captain Liam Cooper, but a little harder with the late withdrawal of Pablo Hernández, who was injured during the warm-up and replaced in the starting 11 by Rodrigo. It would be Cooper's second Premier League appearance, ten years after his first for Hull City, while for Rodrigo it was his first Premier League start in nine years after his earlier spell with Bolton Wanderers. And these two had more Premier League experience than nearly all their team-mates.

It was a bright and sunny afternoon to welcome Premier League football back to Elland Road, but no Leeds fans were there to experience the day we'd waited 16 years for. There weren't even any cardboard cut-outs any more. The 20,000 – including Verne Troyer, Osama bin Laden, and my son, Alessandro – had been discarded, a decision I failed to understand until seeing the blue sheeting that covered every seat, draped in advertising. Ah the modern game, never missing the opportunity to squeeze in some extra revenue. The consolation during the behind-closed-doors era was a suspension of the Saturday 3pm 'blackout', so I was able to watch this landmark game in the Empress pub with my mates. It was my first time watching Leeds in a boozer under the 'New Normal' conditions, and it was a joy to be one step closer to the 'Old Normal', even if we did have to stick to our pre-booked, socially distanced tables.

The first half was a half of two halves. Leeds started on the front foot and took the lead when Hélder Costa smashed the ball in off the bar from a poorly defended corner, then Fulham took control and Aleksandar Mitrović equalised from the spot after Robin Koch needlessly fouled Joe Bryan in the box. Bryan then needlessly gave away a penalty himself, and Klich's super-cool finish handed Leeds a slightly fortunate half-time lead.

The first half of the second half was also a half of two halves. Bamford extended the lead before turning provider, by skinning his marker and pulling the ball back for Costa to thunder it into the top corner, 4-1 to Super Leeds! Yet within ten minutes it was 4-3, then almost 4-4 when Fulham were denied by the post. With a quarter of the game remaining I was braced for disaster, but Leeds dug deep, regained their composure and the final whistle brought an end to 20 minutes of stress, as well as a 198-month wait for a Premier League victory.

With two 4-3 games to start the season Bielsa had announced himself spectacularly, but aired his concerns at the rate Leeds were leaking goals and the freakishly high efficiency in front of goal. Unusually for El Loco, he suggested new signings could be arriving, an admission that was perhaps born from the preceding midweek League Cup defeat to League One Hull. The second string's performance was even more embarrassing than the result, highlighting the need to raise the standard of competition in the squad.

Sheffield United 0 Leeds United 1

Having shipped seven goals in two games, most people wouldn't have been surprised to see Leeds strengthen their defence, especially considering the squad only contained two recognised senior centre-backs in Liam Cooper and Robin Koch. Yet Bielsa had maintained all summer that another defender was not required, because Luke Ayling could shift across from right-back if needed and Pascal Struijk could step up from the reserves (as he had so impressively at Anfield). Alas, there was a rare change of heart from El Loco and Leeds splashed out £18m on a Spanish international centre-back, Diego Llorente from Real Sociedad. Having made no secret of his strategy to target 'the cream of the Championship', it was strange that the three signings brought in by sporting director Victor Orta were all internationals from Europe's top leagues, though nobody was complaining.

My wife, Frankie, Alessandro and I headed to my parents' house to scrounge a free Sunday dinner and capitalise on their BT Sport subscription to watch the first Premier League Yorkshire derby in a staggering 19 years. Leeds had won that match 6-1 against Bradford City and started with aplomb at Bramall Lane, dominating like it was a Championship fixture and playing some brilliant football, yet they would have gone into half-time trailing had Illan Meslier not produced two Nigel Martyn-esque wonder-saves towards the end of the half.

I had been surprised to see Tyler Roberts take Rodrigo's starting place for this match, but for the second half Bielsa switched them back and Rodrigo showed his true quality for the first time. So too did Koch, putting in a colossal performance alongside the ever-reliable captain Cooper, who was making his 200th Leeds appearance. What a milestone for a defender who was written off before Marcelo Bielsa arrived in Yorkshire, and with Cooper having already become an integral part of the Scotland squad, England manager Gareth Southgate must have been pining over the skipper's lost allegiance as he watched from the stands at Bramall Lane.

Southgate must also have been intrigued by the excellent performances of Luke Ayling, Jack Harrison and Patrick Bamford. They'd all made impressive starts to the season, and the latter two combined to snatch all three points at the death and send me and my dad cock-a-hoop. An exhausted Bamford explained afterwards that he'd instructed Harrison to keep putting the ball to the back post, and Jackie's 88th-minute delivery was bang on the money, and bang off Bamford's lovely, wholesome face, which bobbled the ball delightfully into the corner of the net.

Leeds may have had 17 shots and 63 per cent possession, but it had been an end-to-end Yorkshire derby and came as no surprise when their 20-year-old goalkeeper received the man of the match award. Illan Meslier's chance to stake his claim for the number one jersey had come in the most controversial circumstances (a racism ban for his mentor) and at the most pressurised time (the promotion run-in), but his assured performances convinced Bielsa that he could be relied upon in the Premier League and his faith was being repaid. The majority of Leeds's squad was made up of bargain buys – even if most only became bargains once they began working with El Loco – and at £5m Meslier was one of the most expensive players in the squad; nevertheless, plucking him from the reserves of a French second division club appeared to be the shrewdest of Victor Orta's many signings since joining the club in 2017. He already looked to be one of the best young goalkeepers in Europe.

October 2020

Bryn Law – 'Football behind closed doors was bizarre; watching the games when you can hear every call of the players is very, very odd. But from a professional perspective, the most crucial part of the day – the logistical process – became the simplest of processes. You could drive straight up to the ground and park right outside, and quite a few ex-pros would remark about how much they enjoyed there not being any fans! They rock up, watch a game, give their expert opinion, then they can jump in their cars and be home an hour earlier.'

6.	C. Palace	6
7.	LEEDS	6
8.	Tottenham	4
9.	Chelsea	4
10.	Newcastle	4
11.	West Ham	3

Leeds United 1 Manchester City 1

The transformation of the Premier League since the Damned United's exile into the wilderness had been evolutionary rather than revolutionary. Money had been controlling football since Sky introduced 'a whole new ball game' in 1992, and by 2004 there was a clear top order: Manchester United, Arsenal, Liverpool and Chelsea. By 2020 this had evolved into a 'Big Six', thanks to excellent management by Daniel Levy at Tottenham Hotspur, and excellent spending by Sheik Mansour at Manchester City.

The transformation on the blue side of Manchester since oil money arrived at the start of the 2008/09 season was certainly revolutionary, and was comically summed up by the fact they had lost their final match of the previous season 8-1 at Middlesbrough. City had been a laughing stock my whole life – if Leeds were the Damned United, this lot were the Damned City – and, like Leeds, they too had dropped to the third tier of English football in recent times, although only for one season thanks to a miracle injury-time double-salvo which enabled them to win the play-off final on penalties (less damned than Leeds then). Money doesn't necessarily equal success but City probably had too much of it to fail, and subsequently had won more in the previous ten years than United had in 100: four league titles to three, two FA Cups to one, and four other major trophies to three.

City had been Leeds's closest rival when the Whites lost their relegation battle in 2004, and the clubs still shared similarities in 2020 (minus the money and the trophies of course). These were two progressive clubs who invested heavily in youth and infrastructure to create the best environment for the first team to prosper, and both were led by coaches whose places in the football history books were already secured. City's manager, Pep Guardiola, was widely regarded as the world's best, but Leeds were led by his idol, the man whose brains Pep flew 6,500 miles to pick before starting out in his managerial career.

Watching Bielsa take on Guardiola on a Saturday evening at Elland Road was the stuff of dreams, and it would remain that way as rising cases of Covid scuppered the government's plan to allow fans back into stadiums by 1 October. This setback made me doubt whether I'd get to a game all season, which darkened my mood significantly. I'd just about managed to come to terms with missing last season's run-in thanks to some redeeming circumstances – the iconic goal that effectively won us promotion came in a match I wouldn't have attended anyway, the goal that actually won us promotion wasn't even in a Leeds game, and the spontaneous promotion party outside Elland Road would have been no different in the Old Normal – but there could be no vindication for missing our first year back in the big time, our reward for enduring 14 years devoid of hope, and two years paralysed by it. So, on matchday I was feeling pretty low as I trudged across The Stray to The Empress, acutely aware that I should have been bouncing down Beeston Hill to Elland Road, where the atmosphere would have been as electric as any European night.

The chasm between these two teams was fittingly summed up by the fact City's new centre-back, Rúben Dias, cost more than Leeds's entire starting 11. It's the type of stat usually reserved for a David vs Goliath cup tie, and for the first 20 minutes that's exactly what this game resembled. Leeds couldn't get the ball or keep it, and such was City's superiority that Raheem Sterling's opening goal after 17 minutes felt a long time coming. Fortunate that their opponents weren't out of sight, Leeds began to settle into the match and three chances came and went before half-time, reminding City they were in a game.

And what a game! Bielsa made two substitutions that transformed it into a ding-dong, end-to-end battle. Ian Poveda, a 20-year-old winger released by City just ten months earlier, came on at half-time and ran rings around Benjamin Mendy until the £50m left-back was finally withdrawn (and replaced by £40m Nathan Aké), and shortly after half-time Rodrigo was introduced and performed exceptionally well in the 'Pablo role'. The record signing was central to all the attacking play and deservedly grabbed the equaliser himself from a corner, when goalkeeper Ederson dropped the ball at his feet, but the Brazilian made amends minutes later by miraculously tipping Rodrigo's brilliant header on to the bar. With both teams going hammer and tongs for all three points, the commentators were again left mesmerised by the wonderful spectacle.

The engrossing action wasn't limited to the pitch either, because the Bielsa vs Guardiola tactical battle lived up to its billing too. El Loco would later praise Pep's 77th-minute substitution – Fernandinho for Riyad Mahrez – which swung the game back in City's favour. It may have looked a defensive move to the untrained eye, but as The Great Man explained, a stronger defence enables you to attack better, and the last ten minutes were largely spent in Leeds territory. The match had followed a similar pattern to the Liverpool encounter, but this time United stood up to the late pressure to claim an impressive point and make one too – Marcelo Bielsa's Leeds United were not happy losers, they had arrived to challenge the elite.

'It was the right result,' Pep said to Marcelo, as they shook hands in the Yorkshire rain after the final whistle. El Loco gazed happily at his counterpart, probably thinking,

'God I'm glad you're not Neil Harris,' but actually saying, 'You think so?' Everyone thought so. Leeds were the hot topic once again as pundits marvelled at the amazing brand of football Bielsa had brought to the Premier League: the numbers his team committed forward, the speed with which they got behind the ball, the movement, the energy, the passion, the aggression, and the revolutionary man-marking system all over the pitch. It was unanimous – Bielsa's Leeds were a breath of fresh air.

Leeds United 0 Wolverhampton Wanderers 1

The transfer window was a brand-new concept when Leeds were relegated in 2004; before then clubs were able to sign players whenever they liked (until the transfer deadline in the spring). Deadline day has thrown up many weird and not so wonderful stories at Elland Road down the years: star strikers appearing live on Sky Sports News to force a move away, new owners being barricaded inside the stadium by angry protesters, and the infamous 'don't go to bed just yet' tweet from the club, which preceded nothing but a youth player exiting on loan.

Leeds did their best to avoid any late shenanigans this time, by agreeing a £20m deal to sign Michaël Cuisance from Bayern Munich in the days before the window 'slammed shut'. However, after an unimpressive medical Bielsa pulled the plug and attention instead turned to Rennes's Brazilian winger, Raphinha. Cue a race against time to get the £17m deal over the line, and amid rising panic the white smoke finally came at 10.30pm on deadline day, via a cheeky nod to the bad old days. 'Don't go to bed just yet,' tweeted the club's official account – Leeds had their man. When asked why he had sacrificed Champions

League football with Rennes, 23-year-old Raphinha explained that he'd been so 'enchanted' watching Leeds's performances against Liverpool and Manchester City that he had to take the chance to join Bielsa's band of brothers. Added to the money committed to making the loans of Meslier and Hélder Costa permanent, plus signings made for the development squad (Joe Gelhardt, Sam Greenwood, Crysencio Summerville and Cody Drameh), owner Andrea Radrizzani's summer spending had now reached £100m. It was an impressive outlay and a sign of lofty ambitions, and next up United would face the modern-day yardstick for promoted teams. Wolves had qualified for Europe in each of their two Premier League seasons since winning the Championship in 2018, aided by their (dodgy but legal) links to Portuguese 'super-agent' Jorge Mendes, which had resulted in half of the Portugal national team emigrating to the Black Country. The way Leeds had started the season, and with the new additions waiting in the wings, it felt like they were primed to follow in Wolves's footsteps.

An appearance on *Monday Night Football* meant an even longer international break than usual, but it also brought the knowledge that three points at Elland Road would move the Whites up to third spot. Sky's Monday coverage had improved immensely over the years – I would often watch the pre-match build-up and post-match analysis, though rarely the games themselves – so I was excited to see Leeds given the full *MNF* treatment. I headed to my uncle-in-law's unoccupied house to escape any distractions from babies or spouses but was horrified by what I saw when tuning in: Jimmy Floyd Hasselbaink in the studio instead of Gary Neville. Neville not being there was a real come-down; my previous hatred for the ex-Manchester United full-back had subsided thanks to his insightful punditry that was always bang on the money, but I hadn't forgiven Hasselbaink for leaving us high and dry for a big fat pay rise at the start of David O'Leary's revolution, and seeing him piggy-back a career off Leeds United enraged me! And if that wasn't bad enough, Sky's trusty EFL co-commentator, Andy Hinchcliffe, was in the commentary box for what must have been his Premier League debut. Were Sky trolling us?

True to form, Hinchcliffe's pre-match pearls of wisdom belonged in the EFL at best. 'Wolves can't just rely on Raúl Jiménez and hope to push on in the second half,' he proudly proclaimed. Yet Wolves had done exactly that throughout last season (they would have finished in the bottom three based on first-half results, and the top three based on second-half results), and his statement would look as stupid at full time as it sounded at kick-off. In the meantime, Leeds flew out of the blocks. Inside the first ten minutes there was a disallowed goal, a rejected penalty appeal, and chances for Bamford, Costa and Rodrigo. An exaggerated injury gave Wolves a couple of minutes' respite, but it didn't take the spring out of the home team's step as they bossed the half with an exceptional performance. Leeds were quicker, sharper, and first to every ball. They attacked incessantly, with white shirts hurtling forward at every opportunity – rotations, interchanges, flicks and tricks – but Wolves's resolute defence would not be breached.

I was buzzing at half-time. It felt like the best football Leeds had ever played, but in the second half they struggled to hit the same intensity levels and the visitors worked themselves back into the game. El Loco continuously bellowed throughout – 'KEEP GOING! KEEP GOING!' – whipping his horses time and again, but as my dad put it in his 'Leeds... Leeds... Leeds!' match report on Facebook, the fireworks had fizzled out and the Whites were spluttering.

The game should have withered away into a 0-0 draw. VAR chalked off a Wolves goal for a marginal offside but otherwise the visitors rarely threatened, until a weak effort by Jiménez took a wicked deflection off the pineapple on Kalvin Phillips's head, reducing Meslier to a spectator as the ball bounced into the opposite corner. Despite setting up camp in Wolves territory the equaliser never truly looked like coming, and thus Leeds suffered the type of frustrating defeat that had been so familiar in the Championship.

How United fared against Wolves had promised to provide the best indication of where the season's aspirations should be set, but reflecting on the game it was difficult to work out what we had learned. I suppose we'd learned that everything we'd learned in the last two seasons under Marcelo Bielsa still applied, and on a disappointing night I was able to take solace from that.

Aston Villa 0 Leeds United 3

In the week leading up to this game, the self-styled 'Big Six' (the currently richest six clubs in the country – Manchester City, Manchester United, Chelsea, Liverpool, Arsenal and Tottenham Hotspur – referred to as the 'Rich Six' from hereon in) thrust themselves into the headlines by unveiling 'Project Big Picture', a plan to 'save' English football. Under their proposals the Rich Six would assume ultimate control of the football pyramid, and when the proposal was swiftly and emphatically rejected it was revealed that talks were ongoing for the Rich Six to leave the English game and join a new European Super League. I found it astonishing that these clubs would have the audacity to attempt to tear up 150 years of football tradition in order to protect their business models, and Marcelo Bielsa's take on the situation was characteristically philosophical: 'If anything describes English football it is Leagues One and Two. It's important not to forget where you came from.'

Leeds and Aston Villa were precisely the type of clubs the Rich Six were worried about – two massive, historic clubs with the potential to challenge the current top order. But who was bigger? Well, Leeds of course! Villa had more trophies, but they'd never dominated the English game like Leeds did in the 1960s and '70s. Villa also had a bigger stadium, but they didn't have the global following of Leeds, and while the Midlanders had spent more years in the top flight, unlike the Whites they hadn't challenged at the top end of the table since the first Premier League season. Until now? Dean Smith's men were the only team in the country with a 100 per cent league record and fresh from a sensational seven-goal humiliation of Liverpool and a late 1-0 victory at Leicester (another club that had the Rich Six sweating), so just a draw tonight would send them to the top of the league ahead of Everton (another threat to the Rich Six; you can see why they were trying to pull up the drawbridge).

The Wolves defeat had turned into a double whammy, because Kalvin Phillips had injured his shoulder in injury time and would now be sidelined for six weeks. Phillips was the only player in the Leeds squad who was practically irreplaceable, something Bielsa had acknowledged at the start of his reign, admitting, 'It's hard to find another player who can do the same job as Phillips. The best thing for us is if Phillips can play all the games.' Pascal Struijk was tasked with the impossible job of replacing Phillips, but Jack Grealish successfully got the Dutch rookie booked early on and Bielsa immediately substituted him to protect the team from a possible red card (or an inevitable red card, considering Grealish's obsession with winning free kicks and getting players booked). At this point, to describe Leeds as 'patched up' would be an understatement, yet the neutral would have had no idea this wasn't United's settled, first-choice line-up, as they dominated Villa with El Loco's irresistible brand of football.

Half-time bagels brought comparisons with the Wolves game (a great performance with nothing to show for it), and the comparisons might have continued if Grealish had found the net rather than the big frame of Illan Meslier, having dribbled all the way from his own penalty area into and around Leeds's. Instead, a couple of minutes later Leeds took the lead when Patrick Bamford pounced on a rebound inside the six-yard box. Ten minutes after that my jaw was on the floor as Bamford scored the type of goal you would only expect to see from the cream of world football. With little backlift from 20 yards, he struck the ball so sweetly with his instep that it flew into the top corner, via a little kiss off the bar, before the keeper could move. Bamford was officially on fire, and ten minutes later more mesmeric football led to Bamford receiving the ball in the box with his back to goal and surrounded by four defenders. A little pirouette, a shimmy of the hips, and a delicate dink beyond the dive of Emi Martínez sealed a thoroughly magnificent hat-trick for Patrick.

I was again watching in The Empress with my mates, in our regular spot with a prime view of the biggest telly. The experience was as enjoyable as ever, and appreciated more than ever as Harrogate was one of the few places in the country that remained in Tier One, with lower levels of Covid restrictions that allowed people to go to the pub together. Our state of ecstasy after Bamford's hat-trick goal was abruptly broken when, out of nowhere, the manageress came bouncing over, accused us of being rude to the waitress, chucked us out and barred us! We were aghast, but soon realised that Terry's 'cut-throat' gesture to the bar to cancel a round of shots might have been misinterpreted. Amid the furore, the visitors were running riot at Villa Park. We cheekily watched the final ten minutes through the window as United eventually clocked up a whopping 27 shots on goal, and even in the 95th minute Leeds had seven players sprinting upfield on a counter-attack. There were no more goals, but 3-0 was easily enough for a joyous walk home.

By Monday morning you would have been forgiven for thinking the Rich Six had already left the Premier League. Only Liverpool were present in the top eight, and such were Leeds's performance levels I was starting to wonder whether Bielsa could achieve the inconceivable and actually win the Premier League this season!

November 2020

Bryn Law – 'At this point I was the luckiest guy alive from the Leeds fans' perspective, because I was one of the only people given the chance to watch the games. So there was a pressure to make it sound as close to what people recognise as a Premier League game as possible, but without ever being able to really achieve that because the most important element was missing: the fans.'

6.	LEEDS	10
7.	Southampton	10
8.	C. Palace	10
9.	Wolves	10
10.	Chelsea	9
11.	Arsenal	9

Leeds United 1 Leicester City 4

The last team to win the Premier League completely out of the blue was Leicester City. They achieved it in 2016 with a team of players who had previously been written off by their various clubs, or were totally unproven in England's top division. So it could be done! Leicester then endured the worst top-division title defence since Leeds's 17th-placed finish in the inaugural 1992/93 Premier League season, but the Foxes were now enjoying renewed success under Brendan Rodgers and had narrowly missed out on Champions League qualification in the previous season. In fact, many people believed the current Leicester side was better than the one that won the title, so this would be a stiff test for Bielsa's Blue-Arsed Flies.

In the aftermath of 'Waitressgate', crisis talks were held and our ban from The Empress was overturned. Regardless, we had no appetite to return to the scene of the 'crime' and, despite a second lockdown looming due to sky-rocketing Covid cases, I would spend this game like I would spend the rest of November, sat at home. The Whites once again had the chance to go third with victory on *Monday Night Football*, and Bielsa looked set to suffer his first selection headache at Leeds until the team news revealed the unexpected absences of Rodrigo (who became the first United player to contract Covid) and Raphinha, which left El Loco with the type of selection headache he'd become accustomed to in Yorkshire – how to fill a bench.

The first half was a real slog, but it could have been so different had Bamford not headed a sitter straight at Kasper Schmeichel in the opening seconds, or if, from Schmeichel's subsequent distribution, Koch had passed back to Meslier instead of straight to Jamie Vardy. Consequently it was Leicester who led after a minute, and with driving rain saturating the Elland Road pitch, the treacherous conditions coupled with the pace and quality of Vardy seemed to unsettle the Leeds defence, and trepidation quickly reverberated throughout the team. The game was played predominantly in Leicester territory, but every Leeds attack was littered with errors while every

Leicester counter-attack spelt trouble, and by half-time the visitors deservedly led 2-0.

Within minutes of the restart Leeds were on the right side of a huge slice of luck as Stuart Dallas's ball into the box evaded everyone, including Schmeichel, and nestled in the net. Game on! Suddenly Leicester were on the ropes, and Leeds came within inches of an equaliser when Pablo Hernández plucked the ball out of the night sky, shifted it on to his right foot and curled a beauty from 25 yards that Schmeichel could only watch crash off the angle of post and bar. Had that gone in Leeds would have been favourites to win, but rising hopes were soon dashed by dangerman Vardy, who killed the game off after another clinical counter.

In the last minute a marginal VAR-awarded penalty added a sting to the disappointment of the loss. The final score of 4-1 felt a cruel outcome after a spirited comeback attempt, but this result would not cause panic. Brendan Rodgers had built a very good team, solid and efficient, who had done a similar job on Manchester City by winning 5-2 at the Etihad with only 30 per cent possession (they'd had 33 per cent at Elland Road). Even still, it was disconcerting to think other Premier League teams would adopt the same containing tactics, further blunting a Leeds attack that often lacked a cutting edge in the Championship, while utilising their Premier League attackers to cause far greater problems than Nakhi Wells and Chris Martin would cause in the second tier.

'We have to learn to defend better and to attack better,' said Bielsa. Such a complex character, yet one of The Great Man's greatest virtues was picking out the simple truths.

Crystal Palace 4 Leeds United 1

I was 14 years old and in attendance the last time these sides met in the Premier League, back in January 1998, and the 2-0 victory at Selhurst Park also provided the funniest moment I've ever witnessed at football. Lining up against Leeds that day was their record signing Tomas Brolin, whose career had spectacularly nosedived after arriving at Elland Road. Less than two months after signing the Swede from Parma, manager Howard Wilkinson accused Brolin of 'not pulling his weight' in a 5-0 defeat to Liverpool. But it was his weight that was the problem, not the pulling, and Brolin made only 19 appearances for Leeds over the course of two years which were mostly spent ambling around Europe, either on loan or AWOL. His contract was eventually terminated but he was soon back in the Premier League, on a short-term deal at bottom club Crystal Palace, and faced Leeds in his third game.

Brolin took an early whack on the head to the delight of the travelling fans, and while he was off receiving treatment Leeds opened the scoring, and scored again moments after Brolin returned to the pitch sporting a comically bandaged head, Basil Fawlty style. Then, right in front of the travelling army of Leeds fans, Brolin was dispossessed by Rod Wallace, bringing great cheers from an already giddy away end, and a split second later Gary Kelly's clearance smacked him in the head, knocking his bandage clean off! The away fans went wild, and I was unable to resist joining in with the buoyant chants, thus swearing in front of my dad for the first time, 'YOU FAT BASTARD! YOU FAT BASTARD! YOU FAT BASTARD!'

In stark contrast to that memory, Selhurst Park had been an unhappy hunting ground for the Whites in the Premier League, whether against Palace or their 1990s tenants, Wimbledon. Yet this poor record paled into insignificance compared to Leeds's record in London in recent times, where they had only won once in 24 visits. It was a shambolic return, and in the past year the 'London Curse' had developed beyond just losing games too: a racial slur at Charlton, the ridiculous penalty and red card decision at Millwall, the softest of soft penalties at Fulham, a double handball missed by all officials at QPR, and today the curse dished up the worst offside decision in the history of football.

Trouble was brewing well in advance of kick-off when it was announced that the game would only be screened as a 'pay-per-view' event, at a cost of £14.95. The initiative had been launched a month previous, whereby any game that wasn't selected in the usual television slots was subjected to this surcharge to subsidise the lost matchday revenue stream for Premier League clubs – all proceeds would be going into their pockets, not the broadcaster. Unsurprisingly, the decision caused an uproar from supporters who already paid through the nose for TV subscriptions each year, and who couldn't attend matches and had nothing else to do during these unprecedented Covid times, not to mention the fact many had lost their jobs or livelihoods during the pandemic. Thus, a nationwide boycott was arranged, with supporters donating the money they would have spent on watching the games to local food banks instead. Proceeds ran into the hundreds of thousands, and despite this being the club's first pay-per-view game, the Leeds United Supporters' Trust raised a remarkable £90,000. I regret to report that I wasn't strong enough to join in the boycott and succumbed on matchday, but to remove any guilt I donated the money to the food banks too. Thus, it cost me £30 to watch what turned into one of the most exasperating games I'd ever seen.

Leeds were just starting to take control when Palace opened the scoring with a deflected header that sailed in off the crossbar, but the Whites continued to play their stuff and equalised when Klich's clipped through ball was beautifully lifted over the keeper and into the net by Bamford. VAR was a new phenomenon to me, and I had always dreaded its introduction because I knew it would dilute the magic of the ball hitting the net, and this was one such occasion. I couldn't react until I knew Bamford wasn't offside, but once I'd seen the replay I let out a sigh of joy as the freeze-frame clearly showed Bamford was a yard onside of two defenders. But wait, suddenly my anxiety rose again as there were lines being drawn on the pitch by the geeks in the VAR room at Stockley Park, but only Bamford's outstretched arm was offside (pointing to where he wanted the ball played) so no need to worry, the goal would stand. But wait, to my utter bemusement the referee made that dreaded 'computer says no' box gesture, indicating that Bamford was offside and the goal was disallowed! I was livid, perplexed and dismayed, and poor Alessandro had to be escorted out of the living room amid my uncontrollable rage.

So why was it offside? Because of the new handball rule, obviously! Apparently, you could now score with the area of your arm considered to be above your 'T-shirt line' (how ridiculous can you get?) and Bamford's T-shirt line was adjudged to have been a millimetre or so ahead of the defender. That's only half the story though. Along with arguments about whether the line on Bamford's arm was drawn correctly, or the line on the defender's arm for that matter, there appeared to be another defender who was playing Bamford even further onside, but this guy was ignored! Moments later, Ebere Eze curled a magnificent free kick in off the bar and Leeds were 2-0 down. That bloody London Curse.

The universe gave us some reprieve as Bamford got his goal and Klich his assist, when the two combined again to bring Leeds back into the game, but the Football Gods were only toying with us. Just before half-time a low cross deflected off Costa and somehow flew in off the near post from the tightest of angles; the definition of a freak own goal. Playing at Selhurst Park, in London, and against the Football Gods at their most mischievous, there was no hope of turning it around in the second half.

Leeds continued to control possession after the break, but Palace made the best chance and it was duly converted by André Ayew, in off the woodwork just like the other three goals. The contest was over but there was still time for one final insult, when Leeds were denied a stoppage-time penalty because, despite being half in the area, the defender had kicked the part of Bamford's body that wasn't in the area. It may sound trivial but a converted penalty would have kept Leeds above Manchester United on goal difference; instead, a miserable afternoon ended with the Whites below their cross-Pennine rivals in the Premier League table for the first time in over 6,000 days.

Actually, the final insult came when I looked at my bank statement the following day and realised BT Sport had charged me £39.90! This took my exasperation to new levels, and only after numerous emails and phone calls did I finally get the extra £24.95 refunded. Thankfully it would be the last time I'd have to wrestle with BT and my conscience. The voice of the fans had been heard and there would be no more pay-per-view matches. Now all we had to worry about was the back-to-back heavy defeats, and the heavyweight opponents to come: Arsenal, Everton and Chelsea.

Leeds United 0 Arsenal 0

International breaks are difficult at the best of times, but at the worst of times they're hell, and this international break coincided with the beginning of the second nationwide lockdown. As my job was unaffected by the pandemic I was far more fortunate than most, and the initial lockdown had, quite frankly, had numerous upsides, all aided by unseasonably glorious weather. By now though the novelty had well and truly worn off. The thought of a winter lockdown was daunting, and the realisation that we were back to square one was thoroughly depressing.

During the first lockdown I'd set myself the challenge of running 5km in 20 minutes by the time the football season resumed, and clocked a gut-wrenching 20:02 on the morning of 'Project Restart'. If at first you don't succeed, move on to something else, so this time my goal was running a marathon by the time I next attended a Leeds game. How long I had to achieve this was anyone's guess. A Covid vaccine was on the horizon but there was still no indication of when the behind-closed-doors era may end, and everyone was bracing themselves for a full season played in empty stadiums. The Leeds players would often talk about their extra motivation to stay in the division so the fans could enjoy Premier League football next season, though Victor Orta went one step further, claiming he would jump in the River Aire if Leeds were relegated before supporters returned to Elland Road.

Despite not being able to attend the games, and the concerning run of only one win in five, I was enjoying life in the Premier League much more than I thought I would. We had spent so long in the EFL that I'd developed Stockholm Syndrome; like a hostage warming to their captors I became brainwashed into thinking the Championship was the place to be.

The competitiveness and unpredictability, the thick and fast fixture list, and the absence of VAR even led me to call for promotion to be scrapped! When I read up on Stockholm Syndrome (to check the reference was valid) one paragraph spoke of 'learned helplessness', and I definitely had that. Even after promotion I sincerely believed I would miss the Championship and remain a regular viewer of *EFL on Quest*, but now that we were returned to our rightful home I barely even glanced at the Championship results; it just seemed totally irrelevant.

Leeds vs Arsenal is a big match in the English calendar, and this was a big match for Leeds. Questions were being asked of Bielsa's tactics which, although dazzling, had resulted in the joint worst defensive record in the division. In his pre-match press conference El Loco delivered one of his trademark long answers in relation to the defensive issues, with 15 minutes spent dissecting the types of goals Leeds conceded.

The Great Man wasn't concerned, but although my faith in him was unwavering, I was a little concerned. I knew another defeat would amplify the noise around the club and that wouldn't be good for the players, or my mental health. Thus, I was desperate for a result and spent Sunday anxiously waiting for 4.30pm, although by 3.30 the team news had lightened my mood. Kalvin Phillips was back, thrust straight into the starting 11 after five weeks out, and with the Yorkshire Pirlo at his peerless best Leeds looked a different team. Following 20 minutes of nip and tuck United took control of the game, and by half-time they had recorded more shots than any team in a first half so far that season, but hadn't found the net.

Shortly into the second half VAR caught Nicolas Pépé laying a soft head-butt on Gjanni Alioski, leading to a red card for the Arsenal man. This would make it no easier to break the visitors down but Leeds set about their task admirably, aided by the same substitutes that so positively impacted the Manchester City game. Ian Poveda provided the trickery out wide that, in Bielsa's words, could 'unbalance an opponent', while Rodrigo added guile to the midfield, and the bombardment of the Arsenal goal intensified. Rodrigo's 25-yard rasping drive flew inches wide of the top corner, and with another opening from the same position, Rodrigo sacrificed power for accuracy and was only denied by the angle of post and bar. As the clock ticked down Bamford's header hit the inside of the post, and in the 95th minute Raphinha hit the outside of the same post from ten yards. Leeds had been denied by the woodwork on three occasions, having conceded four goals off the woodwork in the previous match. You could almost hear the Football Gods cackling.

Failing to find the net from 25 shots was frustrating, but any point against one of the Premier League's Rich

Six is a good point and I was delighted with how well Leeds had played.

Their results resembled a newly promoted team doing well, but their performances resembled a Champions League team struggling to get going, and I was sure the victories would soon begin to flow. I was also delighted with the clean sheet, United's 41st in 101 league games under Bielsa, which, ironically, was more than every other club in England's top four divisions. Not bad for a defensively naive coach!

Everton 0 Leeds United 1

One person will always spring to mind when Everton and Leeds are mentioned in the same sentence: Gary Speed. Like me, Speed's first love was Everton; unlike me, he joined Leeds's academy, broke into the first team, won promotion back to the top flight, formed part of an iconic midfield quartet that won the last First Division title in 1992, left for his boyhood club in 1996 and went on to make a record-breaking 535 Premier League appearances, then managed his country. Speed was a complete footballer: quick, combative, creative, a clinical finisher, and formidable in the air. He was also a model professional: fit as a fiddle, never injured, passionate, determined and ambitious. And a bloody handsome chap too!

There have been three occasions in my life that left me wondering whether there might actually be some higher power in the universe (beyond those bastard Football Gods), and all of them have come at football. The first game after Speed's tragic suicide was against Nottingham Forest, where the Leeds fans paid tribute to their former number 11 by chanting his name for 11 solid minutes. The very moment the chant ended, Leeds scored with a left-footed, 25-yard piledriver; a goal from heaven. The first game back at Elland Road was so emotional it can still bring me to tears – Gary McAllister, David Batty and Gordon Strachan in funeral attire, carrying flowers to the centre circle with Speed's wife and young boys watching on. Utterly heartbreaking. But at the same time comforting, to know we are part of such a huge and loving family. Scenes such as these prove that football is not just a game. It feels flippant to call it a religion, but it can give you that inner strength when you need it the most.

Having won the 2019 FIFA Fair Play award, Marcelo Bielsa had now been nominated for the 2020 Best FIFA Football Coach honour. The recognition El Loco received while working in the second tier of English football was unprecedented, and sections of the obnoxious British media were typically outraged, which hadn't gone unnoticed by Bielsa. When asked about his nomination The Great Man was typically modest, pointing out that it was a reflection on the staff and players, and the despair Leeds United had suffered over the years, before adding, 'To be nominated is a distinction. It can also be considered excessive. I appreciate all the recognition and I accept all the criticism.'

Bielsa came a very respectful third, behind winner Jürgen Klopp and Bayern Munich's treble-winning manager Hansi Flick. The Argentine was keeping worthy company, and the Saturday evening fixture at Goodison Park brought him up against one of the most revered managers in the world, Carlo Ancelotti. The Italian had won almost every major honour in Italy, Spain, France,

Germany and England, and a few Champions Leagues along the way too, and a year into his latest project Ancelotti was building an exciting Everton team. He'd turned Dominic Calvert-Lewin into a top-class striker, and with the South American flair of Richarlison and James Rodríguez in support, Everton looked the real deal. This would be another huge test for Leeds.

What transpired was special. Leeds went hell for leather at their opponents straight from the kick-off, attacking relentlessly until Everton managed to grab a breather when Luke Ayling took a heavy knock. I had a glance at the clock and couldn't believe we were only three minutes in! The following 87 minutes remained just as enthralling as Everton struggled to cope with Leeds's intensity; only wasteful finishing kept the flowing attacks at bay. Raphinha couldn't convert when clean through, Bamford hit a glaring chance straight at Pickford, and Harrison slid one great chance wide, saw another cleared off the line, and another bounce off the post. But it wasn't all one-way traffic. Everton had chances of their own, forcing Meslier into some terrific saves and beating him twice, only to be denied by the offside flag on each occasion.

The second half brought similar action, and by the final whistle there had been 37 shots but only one goal, which came with 11 minutes remaining, just when it seemed Leeds's energy levels were finally starting to wane. Raphinha picked up the ball 25 yards from goal and looked to his left, expecting to see Gianni Alioski and Stuart Dallas bombing up the wing. For the first time all night there was little support, so the Brazilian had a dig, firing a thunderbolt that skidded past Jordan Pickford into the bottom corner. Alessandro had just been put to bed but I couldn't control my emotions and let out a yelp of joy, what a goal!

Raphinha had been superb all night: quick, direct, clever, tricky, and now he had scored a stunning winner, but that wasn't enough to be named man of the match, nor were Meslier's eight saves, because of Kalvin Phillips's world-class display. His range of passing, reading of the game, tackles and interceptions; it was a near perfect performance, a true midfield masterclass.

'It was a fair result'. El Loco had said the same after most of the games this season, but tonight it was an understatement. The grand statement had already been delivered by his team, to the critics who doubted Bielsa's tactics at this level, and the gutter pundits who claimed Bielsa was not a worthy nominee for the FIFA award. How wrong could they be? Eight of the ten outfield players who started this game, and the 0-0 draw against Arsenal, had been in Bielsa's very first Leeds team. They were average Championship players back then; now they had clocked up 48 shots in two matches against two top Premier League teams, and not conceded a goal. It was an epic feat of pure coaching, the likes of which had never been seen in the modern game.

December 2020

Bryn Law – 'I got completely sucked into the concept of Bielsaball, to the point where I would watch other teams and expect half a dozen players to be sprinting into the opponents' box ten seconds after defending a corner. When it didn't happen I couldn't understand it – "What are you doing? Why are you still dawdling around on the edge of your box? You should be up the other end!"'

7.	Wolves	17
8.	Everton	16
9.	Man Utd	16
10.	Aston Villa	15
11.	Man City	15
12.	LEEDS	14

Chelsea 3 Leeds United 1

Wednesday, 2 December was a momentous day in the battle against Covid-19 as the UK became the first country in the world to approve a vaccine, and the roll-out could begin right away. It was the first significant step forward, back to the Old Normal. This was also the day the second nationwide lockdown ended, and the day that (some) supporters returned to (some) English football stadiums. A maximum of 4,000 fans were allowed in stadiums situated in Tier One-restricted counties, with 2,000 allowed in Tier Two, but stadiums in Tier Three would remain closed. Sadly, Elland Road (along with most of the north) was in Tier Three, yet the club felt confident enough to publicise their plans for welcoming fans back, confirming that season ticket holders would be placed in a ballot per game as soon as West Yorkshire moved into Tier Two. Nothing had really changed, but this gave me such a lift. I'd practically written off my chances of seeing a game before the end of the season, but with a bit of luck I could be back at Elland Road before the end of the month!

Chelsea fans were the last to see Leeds grace the Premier League, and with Stamford Bridge handily placed in Tier Two they would be the first to see their return. It added to what was already a big occasion, the resumption of Chelsea and Leeds's fierce and historic rivalry, which originated (like so much does) from the glory years in the 1960s and '70s under Don Revie. My first visit to Stamford Bridge, in December 1997, was another occasion that felt touched by a higher power. Revie's captain, Billy Bremner, had died a few days earlier at just 54 years of age, and in an emotionally charged first half United embodied the 'Dirty Leeds' label that had been placed upon Bremner and his team-mates by the media. As a result, six players were booked and another two sent off during a goalless opening 45. Nine-man Leeds were cheered down the tunnel by the travelling fans, but in the changing room perhaps there was a divine team talk by Wee Billy, because in the second half the visitors displayed the virtues that Bremner actually stood for. They sweated blood, ran through walls, and kept fighting until the final whistle, thus securing a 0-0 draw that couldn't have honoured Billy's memory any better. 'His hair is red and fuzzy and his body's black and blue, but Leeds go marching on!'

The matches against Liverpool and Manchester City had felt like novelty occasions somewhat, but we were now ten games into the Premier League season and the Whites sat in the top two for many of the important metrics: shots, chances, passes, tackles, interceptions, sprints, distance covered and clean sheets. As a result, this felt like the first time Leeds had faced a major rival as equals in 20 years, and if they could win at Stamford Bridge they would announce themselves as a real force to be reckoned with. To do so they'd need to beat a team whose substitute goalkeeper cost £25m more than Bielsa's starting 11 combined, a team with top spot in their sights and the backing of 2,000 partisan supporters.

Even more spice was added to this fixture due to the man in the opposite dugout, Frank Lampard, who had launched the infamous 'Spygate' fiasco with his cry-baby antics after Bielsa sent an intern to observe his Derby team's training session. Lampard then failed to shake Bielsa's hand after Derby's thrilling victory in the 2019 Championship play-offs, dancing around the Elland Road pitch until El Loco finally gave up waiting by the tunnel, wrong to assume Lampard would show a shred of grace, decency or professionalism. Both managers played down the rivalry but the Leeds fans, and maybe even the players, would never forgive Lampard for the disrespect he had shown The Great Man.

Spending all of Saturday waiting for an 8pm kick-off was tantalising, but it was a start worth waiting for.

Within a minute Meslier was forced into a smart save with his feet, a minute later Olivier Giroud missed a free header from six yards, and a minute after that Kalvin Phillips curled an exquisite ball around the back of the Chelsea defence with his weaker left foot, perfectly weighted for Patrick Bamford to latch on to, round the goalkeeper and hit the back of the net. There was barely time to celebrate though as the action kept coming. Robin Koch limped off injured before Chelsea's struggling £50m striker, Timo Werner, somehow blocked a goalbound header by trying to prod it over the line himself. It was a miraculous let-off, but just as Leeds were finding their feet Giroud found the equaliser, and after an end-to-end last 20 minutes the half ended with the game finely poised at 1-1.

It was all to play for going into the second half, but Leeds were making a habit of losing the pivotal moments in matches and did so again when Raphinha missed a glorious chance to restore the lead, firing over a gaping net with the Chelsea keeper on the floor. Shortly after that, Kurt Zouma was left free at a corner to head the home side into the lead, and once behind, the visitors started to tire.

'PHILLIPS, KEEP MOVING!' Hearing Bielsa's touchline instructions was one positive of the behind-closed-doors era (and doesn't say much for Chelsea's support!), yet they were to little avail this evening as his team struggled to stay in the match. But stay in the match they did, thanks to the brilliant goalkeeping of Meslier and the poor finishing of Chelsea, and if Ian Poveda had not been so honest as to stay on his feet United would surely have been awarded a late penalty and probably snatched a 2-2 draw. Instead, Christian Pulisic (another

Chelsea substitute who cost more than Bielsa's entire team) sealed the victory in the last minute of injury time, sending Lampard wild on the touchline.

Although Leeds had battled admirably, in the end it was a humbling defeat that claimed a large chunk of my optimism. Chelsea were clearly far superior and I had to accept that Bielsa's boys wouldn't be challenging for the title this year, regardless of how good their stats looked.

Leeds United 1 West Ham United 2

In his pre-West Ham press conference, Marcelo Bielsa casually revealed that Diego Llorente had picked up an injury during his debut at Chelsea and would be unavailable until after Christmas. It was a cruel blow for the Spaniard, who had just returned to training after an injury sustained in his first week at Elland Road but was forced into playing more minutes than he was ready for thanks to the injury to Robin Koch, which, incidentally, would keep the German sidelined for three months.

Journalists were conditioned to expect managers to bemoan their bad luck, a packed fixture schedule, or only being allowed to make three substitutions when delivering such news, but there was none of that from El Loco, and when he was subsequently asked whether Leeds would look to sign a defender in January, Bielsa was a little bemused. He calmly explained that another centre-back wouldn't be needed as Phillips or Ayling would play there, but, totally misreading The Great Man, a journalist then asked if he was trying to keep West Ham guessing. Bielsa was now perplexed, and proceeded to name his team, 'Dallas, Ayling, Cooper, Alioski, Meslier, Phillips, Klich, Rodrigo, Raphinha, Bamford and Harrison.' The way he reeled the names off while deep in thought made me wonder whether he was picking his team rather than just naming it. Either way, Stuart Dallas must have been buzzing; he was now officially the first name on the team sheet!

It was a Friday night kick-off at Elland Road and with lockdown lifted we piloted a new pub, The Cricketers in Knaresborough. Barker arrived early enough to secure the best seats in the house – with the help of a landlady who was at the opposite end of the friendliness spectrum to the nutter from The Empress – but Justin and Huddersfield Bill weren't allowed on our table as Covid regulations stipulated that people could only frequent pubs in pairs. They sat in the comfy armchairs instead, in front of a roaring fire and next to the Christmas tree. The only thing missing was the chestnuts; it was a far cry from Elland Road.

Within two minutes of kick-off the serenity was broken by a penalty awarded to Leeds. Klich's weak effort was saved, but VAR spotted Łukasz Fabiański an inch off his line and Klich's retake successfully found the opposite corner. It was another perfect start but, like against Chelsea, there was little time for celebration as West Ham proceeded to tear through the defence almost at will, and eventually equalised from a poorly defended corner, which had become something of a bad habit.

El Loco freshened up both wings at the break, but West Ham were happy to sit back and soak up the pressure as Leeds struggled to penetrate. At this point I really felt the lack of fans was a significant loss. Apart from giving our players an extra boost, the atmosphere might have unsettled West Ham, but in sterile conditions their confidence grew as they realised they could handle what the Whites were throwing at them. Thus, it was no great surprise when the visitors took the lead 15 minutes from time, and certainly no surprise that the goal came from another poorly defended set piece. Now West Ham's confidence was soaring, but a string of superb saves by Meslier kept Leeds in the game, and the Frenchman's heroics would have earned his team a point had Rodrigo's injury-time six-yard header been directed into the net instead of Fabiański's gloves.

With that the game was up, and after an impressive start to the season Leeds had now won only two games in seven, coinciding with the absence of Pablo Hernández. By extreme coincidence, exactly the same had happened in each of Bielsa's first two seasons, and both times United had gone on to win the next seven league games on the bounce once 'El Mago' was restored to the team. It would cause quite the stir if Leeds managed to do that again, although, with pressure rising, just one win would do for now.

Leeds United 5 Newcastle United 2

Marcelo Bielsa was again on great form for his pre-Newcastle presser, which was dominated by questions about Leeds's vulnerability at set pieces. Bielsa explained that his team wasn't conceding an 'exaggerated' number of goals in this manner, but he did admit his defenders were suffering from having their runs blocked off by opponents, a tactic he would not resort to himself. 'Respecting the rules is not being naive,' he reasoned, and with only a matter of days left as the reigning FIFA Fair Play champion, El Loco was signing off in style.

Bielsa was also quizzed on Leeds's poor form and accepted that four points from 18 available was a 'negative cycle', while pointing out that half the teams in the Premier League had gone through a similar run. This negative cycle had me glancing over my shoulder at the bottom of the table for the first time this season, and though Bielsa's words quelled my simmering fears, points speak louder than even The Great Man's words, and anything less than three against Newcastle on Wednesday night would amplify the fears of a jittery fanbase.

There were no changes to the line-up in spite of the worst performance of the season against West Ham, and Leeds started like a team sliding towards the relegation zone. Newcastle were no great shakes, but they looked a cut above in the opening ten minutes and opened the scoring during Leeds's best spell of the half. What a kick in the teeth. Maybe we weren't good enough for the Premier League? But Leeds responded impressively, pressing and probing, and finally equalising when Bamford nodded into an empty net after Rodrigo's looping header had hit the bar. It was no less than the home team deserved, and by half-time they had broken their own record for most shots in a first half this season. The bar was now set at 14.

There was no change in momentum in the second half, although there was a lucky escape when VAR decided not to award a penalty after Liam Cooper clearly and obviously fouled Callum Wilson in the box. Minutes later, Rodrigo spread the ball out wide to Harrison, who majestically controlled the overhit pass with his big toe, then drilled a volleyed cross back to Rodrigo, who arrived in the box to head perfectly into the far corner. A quite outrageous goal. But the lead lasted for just four minutes, and to compound my annoyance the equaliser came from another free header from a corner. While I once again wondered whether this was a sign of struggles to come there were no such fears from Leeds, who continued to 'trust their swing' and soon enough Stuart Dallas had restored the lead. What a relief!

It had been six weeks since Pablo Hernández threw his black armband to the ground in frustration when substituted against Leicester. The following week he was dropped from the squad and, much to the concern of the fanbase, he hadn't featured since. Pablo was the most influential player at the club – only a few months earlier he'd dragged Leeds to promotion with a series of magnificent performances and magical moments – but rumours were rife that his Leeds career was as good as over. Thus, it was a delight to see El Mago return to the fold, charged with helping Leeds over the winning line. In Bielsa language, this doesn't mean keeping the ball in the corner or running down the clock, and within six minutes of coming on Hernández had done what he had been brought on to do: create the goals to take Leeds out of sight.

In an ironic twist of fate, both goals came from Newcastle corners. The first corner led to a six-on-two counter-attack as Leeds showcased their superhuman fitness levels. Pablo chose to feed Gjanni Alioski and the Macedonian left-back finished with aplomb. From the second successfully defended corner Pablo released Jack Harrison. With 'only' three men streaming forward in support, Harrison carried it alone before drilling a sensational 25-yard drive into the top corner, an absolute screamer to cap a stunning 5-2 win.

What a response this was by Leeds; I was absolutely buzzing after the match. I'd like to say the joy was unbridled but in the back of my mind I couldn't help imagining what it would have been like to experience the game from the Kop, where the celebrations for each of the four second-half goals would have been wilder than the last, rather than sat on my own in the kitchen. We had missed a true Elland Road classic, but at least I had seen such classics before. Many of our fans hadn't seen Leeds play Premier League football in their entire lives and it was those I felt most sorry for.

Manchester United 6 Leeds United 2

How things had changed at Old Trafford since Leeds United's Premier League exit. Following the retirement of Alex Ferguson in 2013, our bitterest rivals had become the biggest joke in football (certainly since Bielsa resurrected Leeds anyway) by consistently boasting one of the world's most expensive squads, which was bursting with over-hyped mercenaries and usually competing in the Europa League, rather than UEFA's premier competition, the Champions League. Ole Gunnar Solskjær was the latest man charged with restoring their pride, yet despite pipping Leicester to fourth place last season they were already back in the Europa League after elimination at the Champions League group stage. You love to see it.

Leading up to the 'War of the Roses', Marcelo Bielsa summed up the mood very nicely when he said, 'Ask a Newell's [Old Boys] fan if they want to be champions or beat Rosario Central, they'll say be champions. But if you ask the day before the derby game, they would prefer to win the game. That's exactly how I feel!' El Loco was beaming in his presser, and chuckled as he delivered his pearls of wisdom – I don't think I'd ever seen him as excited for a game. Playing your enemy does bring a unique feeling, one that I'd been denied of almost my entire adult life. It's not as anxiety-provoking as a promotion battle but it's just as intense, and resulted in a 4.30am wake-up and subsequently a painful 12-hour wait for the *Super Sunday* kick-off. I headed round to Rick's after lunch, where a couple of beers and a hundred jokes calmed the butterflies in my stomach. 'Remember in 1995 when we were 2-0 down after four minutes?!' How we laughed.

In his wonderful book, *Love Hurts*, Neil Jeffries compared that 1995 FA Cup tie to root canal work without anaesthetic. Well, today was like having open heart surgery without anaesthetic. Leeds were 2-0 down within three minutes this time, with both goals scored by Scott McTominay after he marauded through a non-existent midfield. Bamford missed a great chance to get Leeds back in the game and then it was 3-0, and then it was 4-0, and only 37 minutes were on the clock. I couldn't believe what was happening. Not in my wildest nightmares had I imagined this scenario, yet at half-time I couldn't help thinking we weren't out of it as Liam Cooper had pulled it back to 4-1. 'Scum will shit themselves if we score the next goal,' was my optimistic take on a dire situation.

We were so close to finding out if my prophecy would ring true, so close that I was off the sofa and celebrating as Raphinha's volley was palmed into the air by David de Gea and seemed to bounce in off the far post. Only it hadn't bounced in, somehow it had bounced out, and Rick punched me in the arm for getting him falsely excited. That was the end of the excitement. Soon it was 6-1 and

Cooper was hobbling off the pitch, meaning all four of Bielsa's centre-backs were now injured (Cooper, Llorente, Koch and Gaetano Berardi). Worse, there was still 25 minutes remaining.

The behind-closed-doors era had already produced some crazy results and I was petrified at how bad this one could become. Thankfully, the Football Gods took mercy on us and Solskjær's side failed to add any further goals. In fact, Leeds actually won the last quarter 1-0 thanks to Stuart Dallas's 25-yard curler into the top corner, and it would have been 2-0 if Jack Harrison hadn't side-footed an injury-time sitter wide of the far post, but this was just damage limitation rather than any consolation.

Although serious pundits like Gary Neville and Roy Keane only had praise for the attitude of Bielsa and his Leeds team, much of the post-match talk was dominated by negative comments about El Loco's tactics, and whether he should consider changing them. Strange really, when those tactics had turned a group of average Championship players into a Premier League team. I chose to assign the blame for this defeat on the players, who had been caught like rabbits in headlights. They'd let the fans down, let themselves down and let Bielsa down, yet they never hid, and fought until the final whistle, and in the circumstances that was truly admirable. The defeat hurt, of course it did, but most Leeds fans were philosophical about it, and knew very well that the man who would be hurting most of all was Marcelo Bielsa.

Leeds United 1 Burnley 0

Just a couple of weeks earlier it had seemed likely that some fans would be returning to Elland Road for this

Boxing Day fixture, but with a new and highly contagious strain of Covid sweeping the nation Christmas was cancelled; a third nationwide lockdown was on the way in early January. Football was back behind closed doors for everyone. My exile from watching Leeds United in the Premier League once again felt destined to extend into an 18th year, which sucked any remaining festive cheer from me, not that there was much left after the pummelling at Old Trafford.

To make matters worse we had to endure a week of the gutter press talking utter dross about Marcelo Bielsa, who was advised to ditch his fearless attacking football and start prioritising results over his philosophy, despite the fact his philosophy had produced the best results by a newly promoted team in recent times. So, it was full Loco mode for the pre-Burnley presser. Two questions brought answers lasting over 40 minutes as Marcelo defended his style of play by running through a detailed analysis of 'The Nightmare Before Christmas'. Frankly, Bielsa could have saved 39 minutes and just used two of his sentences, 'If someone were to analyse the conclusions from a victory to a defeat it would be embarrassing for those who have an opinion. When we win the style is praised, when we lose we are ridiculed.'

Burnley were having a really poor season, but an uptick in form had lifted them out of the relegation zone and this was a game that really concerned me. The Clarets were a direct and physical side, awkward to break down and notorious on set pieces, and with four injured centre-backs I struggled to see how Leeds would cope with an aerial bombardment. Their manager Sean Dyche operated in a good old-fashioned 4-4-2, so Bielsa followed his philosophy and deployed Kalvin Phillips in the middle of a makeshift back three, between right-back Luke Ayling and youngster Pascal Struijk. This tactical shift was always necessary against a front two, as Bielsaball relied upon an extra defender to provide cover in case the man-marking system broke down, so imagine my annoyance when the *Match of the Day* pundits later described this tactical tweak as a pragmatic response to the Old Trafford thrashing. And according to these 'experts' it was Bielsa who was naive!

From the first attack Leeds were given the chance to make the perfect start. Patrick Bamford was upended by the keeper in the box, the referee awarded the penalty and VAR kindly agreed. Having needed a retake to score his previous spot kick, Mateusz Klich relinquished responsibility and Bamford lashed home his tenth goal of the season, a brilliant return from a striker enjoying a new lease of life in the Premier League. But old habits die hard, and for the third time in 2020 Bamford denied Leeds a certain goal by blocking Harrison's shot on the Burnley goal line. Leeds had other chances – it was a superb first-half performance, – but there was a fortunate escape when an equaliser was disallowed for a dubious foul on Illan Meslier, to the fury of the visitors.

In the second half the tables turned; it was backs to the wall throughout. United couldn't find their stride and were entirely reliant on the resilience of their back three to preserve the lead. They challenged for every cross, threw their bodies at every shot, and repelled corner after corner after corner. This was a big three points to protect, but I had no doubt the lads were spurred on by the media's jibes, Bielsa's retort, and the pain of Old

Trafford. They were so determined not to wilt and put in a quite heroic effort.

Screams of delight greeted the final whistle, from the players and staff at Elland Road, and from me in my kitchen. Although it had been horrible to watch, I was delighted with the manner of the victory – the perfect response to the ignorant critics – and delighted for Kalvin Phillips, who had been subbed at half-time at Old Trafford (after spending all week geeing up his team-mates about the importance of the game) but bounced back with an impeccable display at the heart of the defence. But most of all I was delighted for Bielsa, who was never going to change for anyone or anything, and proved as much by moving Phillips back into midfield when Burnley switched to 4-3-3 in the final stages. What a brave move to take our star performer out of a defence under siege. It portrayed the unshakeable belief that The Great Man had in his philosophy, a philosophy that was the whole reason why Leeds United were no longer stagnating in the lower reaches of the Championship.

West Bromwich Albion 0 Leeds United 5

The venue for Leeds's last game of the year was the same as their first. On New Year's Day 2020 there was nothing to separate United and West Brom, whose 1-1 draw at The Hawthorns left them tied at the top of the table, but the clubs had drifted in different directions since escaping the Championship. The Baggies had only won once in 15 Premier League games and sacked their popular manager, Slaven Bilić, while Leeds had established themselves in mid-table with 20 points already on the board, 12 clear of tonight's opponents.

In their desperation to escape the drop zone the Baggies had appointed 'survival specialist' Sam Allardyce to replace Bilić, and fresh from an encouraging 1-1 draw at Liverpool 'Big Sam' was excited about the challenge of facing Marcelo Bielsa. It would be another clash of cultures, not just in the brands of football but also the managers' preparation levels. 'It'll be interesting to see how they play,' remarked Allardyce. 'I've got an idea. I watched them a little bit on the telly against Burnley.' Perhaps he should have spent a few hundred more hours analysing Leeds, although his team still wouldn't have stood a chance, with the Whites, dressed in maroon, at their irrepressible best.

I headed to Nige's to watch this game, my only get-together of the festive period thanks to the restrictions. He'd set up a gazebo in his back yard to provide a comfortable setting while sticking to the Covid guidelines, and although coats and hats were required in near freezing conditions, once the pizza oven got going and the goals started flowing, we were all positively glowing. Nine days earlier Leeds had trailed 4-0 after 40 minutes at Old Trafford; here they led 4-0 after 40 minutes.

The opener was a disastrous own goal, a back-pass that bypassed the keeper straight into the net. The second was a strike of pure quality, in off the far post from the laces of Gjanni Alioski. Then came another beauty to add to Jack Harrison's growing collection; a flowing move, a one-two on the edge of the box, a little Cruyff turn to win half a yard, and a calm finish into the top corner. The fourth goal was aided by a large deflection, but it belonged to Rodrigo and both he and Leeds had earned their luck; 4-0 at half-time flattered nobody. Only one further goal was added in the second half but what a goal it was, a screamer from Raphinha after another beautiful, flowing one-touch move. It should be said that West Brom were possibly the worst team I'd ever seen in the Premier League, but even so, Leeds were sensational.

In keeping with the traditions of the club, good moments always come at a price, and after this breathtaking victory came a media pile-on with Leeds United accused of 'cyber bullying' and initiating a tirade of sexist abuse. The episode was started by match pundit Karen Carney, who questioned the wisdom of Leeds's intensity levels and claimed they had only been promoted because of Covid. Considering the Whites had won five games on the bounce without conceding a goal prior to the suspension of their promotion season, not to mention clearly being one of the best Championship teams of all time (a claim hardened by the impression they had made on the Premier League) it was a pretty wild remark, and the club's Twitter account duly responded by posting a photo of Carney after the match, with the caption, 'Promoted because of Covid, won the league by ten points.'

Any male pundit would have felt the wrath of the Leeds Twitterati for such grossly disparaging comments, but male pundits wouldn't be subjected to the sexist abuse Carney faced, and she eventually deleted her Twitter account in the coming days. Rather than lambast the abusive tweeters, the attitudes of a nation or the social media platform that openly allows this type of abuse and worse, the media's outrage was squarely placed on Leeds United, with the club widely and venomously criticised for opening Carney up to abuse. You could say Leeds were cyber-bullied themselves having actually done nothing wrong (they didn't even tag Carney into the tweet), but it's probably best to simply blame the whole furore on the toxic nature of social media, the modern-day root of all evil!

What a way to end 2020, an infamous 12 months that would always be remembered as the year our dreams came true, in circumstances beyond our wildest imaginations.

January 2021

Bryn Law – 'There's lots of "noise" that surrounds Leeds United – it's always there, it's part of it – and people were never going to be eternally grateful just for having Manchester United on the fixture list instead of Rotherham. Leeds were now perceived as a Premier League club, and if they weren't doing well in the Premier League there was something fundamentally awry.'

6.	Chelsea	26
7.	Tottenham	26
8.	Man City	26
9.	Southampton	26
10.	West Ham	23
11.	LEEDS	23

Tottenham Hotspur 3 Leeds United 0

Leeds were preparing for life outside the Premier League when José Mourinho arrived in England, announcing himself with a line that was misquoted and instantly iconic: 'I am a special one.' Two years later 'The Special One' had delivered Chelsea's first two league titles in over 50 years. I loved Mourinho in those early years (and not just for knocking Alex Ferguson off his perch), but when Pep Guardiola knocked José off his perch he encountered a personality transplant and restyled himself as the anti-Pep, with a demeanour as dour as his football.

In light of all the above, Mourinho was a controversial appointment for Tottenham Hotspur in 2019. Not only was his philosophy at odds with a fanbase who were notorious in their demands for entertaining football, he was also a club legend at a bitter rival. It was a throwback to August 1998, when Tottenham poached Arsenal favourite George Graham from Leeds, a move that only benefitted the party who'd been shafted. Mind you, George did deliver a trophy at Spurs (the League Cup), and I was intrigued to see whether José would fare any better.

In this match, José fared very well. El Loco was without his four centre-backs again, but because he never moaned about it nobody in football seemed to have noticed. Perhaps it was a reflection of how well Leeds were coping. Young Pascal Struijk was proving an assured partner for stand-in captain Luke Ayling, who had taken to his centre-back role as well as he'd taken to the Premier League. Ayling was terrific again on Leeds's first trip to the Tottenham Hotspur Stadium (a stadium so lavish that nobody could afford the naming rights), with his sporadic bursts forward a great weapon for turning defence into attack. Ahead of him, Kalvin Phillips put in a top-class performance against top-class opposition, though beyond that there were few positives. Leeds started full of confidence but chances and half-chances slipped away, and the match changed when a mistake by Meslier led to a mistake by the referee, and then a mistake by VAR, who awarded a penalty despite the video evidence clearly showing Alioski was outside the box when tangling with the Spurs attacker. That bloody London Curse. Harry Kane dispatched down the middle and soon turned provider as Son Heung-min bagged his 100th Tottenham goal to double the lead.

After half-time Leeds's weakness at defending corners was exploited by Toby Alderweireld, whose header killed the game off with 40 minutes still remaining, and that was the most disappointing thing of all. We were still under the third national lockdown and Leeds games were the only thing to look forward to, so to have our entertainment limited to 50 minutes felt so cruel. Seeming to appreciate this, the players never let up and the last 40 minutes was a replica of the first 20 – all Leeds but no goals.

My long-suffering wife was loving life in the Premier League. I'd always promised her that promotion would bring an end to the matchday stresses and strains and, so far, my words were ringing true. In the Championship I was either relieved or devastated at the final whistle, whereas in the Premier League I was either elated or content. Sleepless nights were seldom, all-day anxiety was scarce, and terrifying outbursts during games were few and far between. It was a conscious decision to try and enjoy this season, but with Leeds sitting comfortably clear of the relegation zone the enjoyment came naturally, especially considering the fabulous football on show. Even in this most routine defeat of the season, Bielsa's side still held 64 per cent of the possession and registered 18 shots at goal. For a newly promoted team away to one of the Rich Six those stats were unheard of, but in the Loco way one lives, and loses, better.

Leeds United 0 Brighton & Hove Albion 1

Much fun was made when Brighton categorically refused to sell Ben White to Leeds because they were a 'direct rival'.

Although sprinkled with bravado, the reaction on Twitter was an indication of the pre-season expectations at Elland Road, and those expectations were being met. Brighton were languishing in 17th while Leeds would have to be classed as chasing Europe rather than scrapping against relegation, thanks in part to how terribly the bottom three were doing. Sheffield Utd had just two points on the board (two!), West Brom eight, and Fulham 11, yet it was too early to consider Leeds safe. With 21 games remaining there was plenty of time for things to change, and losing to Brighton would be a bad place to start.

If Leeds were to start sliding down the table nobody would view Brighton as the turning point though, thanks to a calamitous FA Cup defeat the week before. Leeds fielded a strong team away to League Two Crawley Town, but Bielsa severely weakened the side with three half-time changes and by the final whistle a 3-0 defeat was an accurate reflection of yet another disastrous cup tie. In recent years there had been defeats to Histon, Sutton, Hereford, Rochdale and Newport, but these all came when there was no chance of winning the competition; they were embarrassing but not hurtful. Crawley hurt. I'd held high hopes of a glorious cup run, but instead we'd been trounced by a team that brought on a reality TV star for the last couple of minutes. Bielsa and the players owed us for this, and beating Brighton would be a good place to start.

The Brighton game worried me from the moment Kalvin Phillips was booked towards the end of the defeat to Spurs and earned a one-match suspension, because without him Leeds just couldn't seem to control and dominate games, and a possible defeat became probable when Kiko Casilla was named in the starting line-up. The disgraced goalkeeper was at his kamikaze worst at Crawley but retained his place due to Illan Meslier's positive Covid test. At least the form guide appeared to be in Leeds's favour, but the fact Brighton hadn't won in nine matches, and had never won a Premier League game in the month of January, just added to my pessimism. Both runs were due to end, and I braced myself for the worst.

The worst was exactly what we got; the worst performance of the season by far, and possibly even the worst performance under Bielsa. It didn't take long for Brighton to carve open a static defence, with Neil Maupay left all alone to tap into an unguarded net, and the concession failed to spark United into life. They were sloppy and sluggish, with no zip in the passing or pressing, little movement or aggression, one shot on goal, and only four touches for Patrick Bamford through the entire first half. Leeds did improve in the second half but the only player showing any quality was guilty of missing the best opportunity, as Jack Harrison curled wide of the far post when he didn't need to be so accurate. Otherwise, it was all huff and puff from the Whites, and Brighton deservedly ended their long winless run.

Leeds were due to host Southampton in midweek but the fixture fell foul of the contagious new strain of Covid that was decimating Premier League squads, with games being postponed left, right and centre. At this point it felt inevitable that the football season would be halted, which filled me with trepidation. Bielsaball was getting me through these unprecedented times, so no football on top of the continuing lockdown would likely be too much for my mental health to take. Thankfully no hiatus was forthcoming, but there was still a ten-day wait for the next match which, although excruciating, felt like a necessary evil. After such a poor display on the back of successive 3-0 defeats, the break would surely do Leeds good. It would certainly be good for the Elland Road pitch, which hadn't been in a worse state since Hunslet rugby club shared tenancy in the mid-1990s.

'To have lost three games without scoring cannot happen without causing worry.' El Loco was pulling no punches. It had been a bad start to 2021, and with two difficult away games at Newcastle and Leicester to come, concern was knocking at the door once again.

Newcastle United 1 Leeds United 2

We had reached the halfway point of the Premier League season and Marcelo Bielsa surmised, 'If we had a few more points it would not be unjust.' The Great Man wasn't moaning (although it's as close to moaning as you would ever hear from him), just simply expressing a justifiable opinion, and with this in mind I was confident of collecting more points on the back 19 than we had on the front 19. This positive mindset may have been helped by the news of a £30m injection into the club by the San Francisco 49ers, who increased their 15 per cent share to 37 per cent. Just a few short years ago an investment of this size would have been mind-boggling, but thanks to the work of Bielsa this money was just another healthy step forward in the rebirth of Leeds United. And reassuring too, at a time when clubs were struggling financially due to the pandemic.

An end to the three-match losing streak would bring timely reassurance on the pitch, and a midweek trip to beleaguered Newcastle offered the perfect opportunity. Bielsa was able to field two natural centre-backs for the first time in ten weeks, but only for seven minutes as the desperately unfortunate Diego Llorente hobbled off in tears after suffering a hamstring injury. It was gut-wrenching news for the Spaniard, but Leeds had started brightly and continued to dominate a Newcastle side who hadn't won in ten games and looked bereft of any heart or belief.

The visitors took the lead midway through the half when a swift counter-attack was finished off with a touch of quality in the final third, something that had previously been lacking through Bielsa's reign. Rodrigo picked out Raphinha and the Brazilian calmly swept the ball into the corner of the net. It had been a stop-start season for all of Leeds's summer signings, but tonight their Brazilian-born forwards were both superb. Raphinha tormented Newcastle down the wing and Rodrigo dictated everything through the middle, enjoying easily his best game for Leeds.

At half-time Steve Bruce must have suspected he was delivering his final team talk in Premier League management, but the introduction of powerhouse winger Allan Saint-Maximin injected life into his team and changed the game. Leeds seemed shell-shocked by their opponents' rejuvenation and were punished by Miguel Almirón's equaliser, yet they responded immediately, scoring from another trademark counter that swept up the pitch and ended with Harrison beautifully curling a bouncing ball inside the far post with the outside of his left boot. Saint-Maximin continued to terrorise the patched-up defence, but Leeds held firm to return to winning ways.

With 26 points on the board safety was already within sight. In fact, Leeds could afford to lose the last 19 matches and still stay up if the bottom three continued collecting points at the same rate. So, it was back to concentrating on the top half of the table and the nine-point gap to the Champions League spots. After so many years in the doldrums I felt entitled to let myself get a bit carried away.

Leicester City 1 Leeds United 3

Hard to believe perhaps, but when I were a lad the second match I'd look for on the fixture list was Leicester away, such was my loathing of the East Midlanders, their players, their fans, and their poxy ground. These feelings were a culmination of every trip to Filbert Street always ending in catastrophe, but Filbert Street had since been replaced by a new modern stadium, and bloodying the noses of bigger clubs was one of few similarities between the unfashionable Leicester City of the late 1990s and the current incarnation.

'The Leicester model' had become a much-used phrase when discussing strategies to hijack the Premier League's top six. The Foxes bought well, sold well, and had become a team that consistently pushed for European football, and on the eve of this *Super Sunday* clash, Leeds owner Andrea Radrizzani praised the running of the club as an example of how he hoped to restore United to their former glories. Leicester's manager, Brendan Rodgers, was equally complimentary about his opposite number at Elland Road. Rodgers, the best of a bad bunch of British managers (comically, British managers occupied the bottom seven spots in the Premier League), spoke of his admiration for Marcelo Bielsa's philosophy, including his players' integrity in respecting the officials. This was the first time that Leeds's gentlemanly conduct had been complimented, and although it barely caused a tremor in the elite football cesspit, for my dreams of Bielsa saving the sport it was a start.

With Leicester missing the irreplaceable Jamie Vardy I was quietly confident of springing a surprise, but the home side took the lead with an all-too-familiar saunter through the middle of the pitch. The goal did nothing to dampen the spirit of the visitors though, and within minutes Stuart Dallas had brilliantly steered Bamford's through ball past Kasper Schmeichel. Dallas had taken Mateusz Klich's midfield role, with the Pole finally suffering a dip in form after two and a half years cemented in the heart of the side, and I'd doubted whether Dallas could cut it in a Premier League midfield. I'd also doubted him as a Championship winger, right-back and left-back, but his meteoric rise under El Loco's stewardship seemed to know no bounds and today he excelled in another fantastic Leeds performance.

Despite Rodrigo hobbling off shortly after the equaliser, Leeds grew in stature and by half-time I was thrilled by what I'd seen, if a little frustrated not to have capitalised on the dominance. In an attempt to jump-start his misfiring side Rodgers made a tactical substitution that changed the game, but the period Leeds spent against the ropes was the most pleasing aspect of the afternoon for me. The team adapted to the situation, managing the game by making it niggly, doing what was required to get through a difficult period, and then took the lead against the run of play. And what a stunning goal it was. Struijk's tenacity won the ball back in the Leicester half and Raphinha played a crisp pass through to Bamford, who fired a world-class thunderbolt into the top corner, via a little kiss off the bar; an incredible finish. As per usual, I couldn't celebrate the goal until the replay confirmed it wasn't offside, but I was stunned into silence regardless.

Leicester threw everything at Leeds in search of an equaliser, but the visitors' last standing defenders, Liam Cooper and Pascal Struijk, were colossal, and with their last standing new signing (Raphinha) forced off with injury, United finished the game with 11 players who won the Championship the previous season. And they did so expertly, sealing the points with another wonderful counter-attack. Jack Harrison put the ball in the net, but Bamford received the plaudits for handing the goal on a plate for the young winger.

Asked after the game about the beauty of Bamford's wonder strike, Bielsa instead preferred to talk about the beauty of Bamford's selflessness, 'What I value the most is that for the Harrison goal he chose to give the pass. It described Bamford more than anything, that he thinks more about the team than himself.' This is the word of the Lord.

February 2021

Bryn Law – 'I never spoke to Bielsa despite covering nearly every single game over three seasons, which is extremely unusual. My only encounter with him was when I nodded to him in the street in Wetherby, though he probably didn't have a clue who I was! He wouldn't engage with anybody in the media, apart from when he had to, so I had no personal attachment other than loving the football I was watching.'

7.	Chelsea	33
8.	Everton	33
9.	Aston Villa	32
10.	Arsenal	31
11.	Southampton	29
12.	LEEDS	29

Leeds United 1 Everton 2

Back-to-back away wins had rekindled dreams of a chase for Europe, and with six games against six teams immediately surrounding them in the league – Everton, Crystal Palace, Arsenal, Wolves, Southampton and Aston Villa – February had the potential to be a pivotal month in United's season. The January transfer window had passed quietly, as had been expected, and Leeds's only acquisition had spent two weeks bedding in and was all set for its home debut following a £300,000 transfer from Tottenham. It was clear after the Brighton game that time was up for its predecessor, and under the lights at Elland Road the new pitch looked immaculate ahead of the visit of Everton.

As had become the custom in lockdown, I popped to the Co-op for two large bottles of Peroni, one for each half. I settled in the kitchen feeling smug having once again been asked for ID (my face mask must have taken years off me), but the first half served as a real comedown as Leeds's defence was punished for switching off twice – once at the beginning and once at the end – while their attack lacked inspiration. The new pitch was having a poor game too; players were slipping over in almost every attack, which didn't help Leeds's performance or the overall spectacle.

Despite the two-goal deficit there were no changes at half-time, and El Loco's faith in his players paid off. Raphinha halved the deficit within minutes of the restart and triggered an almighty onslaught, yet wave after wave of attacks brought save after save from Everton's stand-in goalkeeper. Still Leeds pushed and pushed, relentlessly running, tackling, pressing and harrying; it was a joy to see, but once again tinged with regret when imagining how vociferously a full Elland Road would have roared the lads on. Whether the Kop would have sucked an equaliser into the net we'll never know, but Tyler Roberts ballooned the last chance of the match over the bar and Leeds's almighty efforts sadly came to nowt.

I was still buzzing after the game regardless of the defeat. The team had done us so proud, and captain

FEBRUARY 2021

Liam Cooper's post-match words reflected the feelings of the fanbase, 'I told the lads that if we're going to lose, that is the way we lose; by giving everything.' It had been yet another pulsating Leeds United match, reaffirming the fact Bielsa's team was the best watch in the Premier League, and Southampton's 9-0 defeat at Old Trafford meant the Whites had overtaken them on goal difference and sat proudly at the top of the bottom half of the table. And I'm always happy when Leeds are top.

Leeds United 2 Crystal Palace 0

Leeds were given the *Monday Night Football* slot yet again, meaning another long wait to see El Loco's team in action. Wall-to-wall live Premier League football consumed the whole weekend (Friday 6pm and 8pm, Saturday 12.30pm, 3pm, 5.30pm and 8pm, Sunday 12pm, 2pm, 4.30pm and 7pm, and Monday 6pm and 8pm) but it was never enough to quench my thirst for Bielsaball. I hadn't really felt like a football fan since I was at school, I was simply a Leeds fan, and having been subjected to Bielsaball I could barely stomach 'normal' football any more.

The jam-packed TV schedule usually left no time for detailed previews or analysis of the matches, though tonight Leeds had the floor to themselves, the only team in action. There was another side due to play at Elland Road, but Crystal Palace never turned up. Within two minutes of kick-off they'd been hounded out of possession in their own half and Harrison thumped in the opening goal via a deflection. Scoring early at Elland Road had become a lovely habit, and from that moment onwards the points never looked in doubt.

Palace's no-show was as much down to the home side as it was themselves. Liam Cooper enjoyed probably his best game in a Leeds shirt, so dominant and composed, he looked every bit a top Premier League defender. It may have been Stuart Dallas's best game in a Leeds shirt too – certainly his best in the midfield as he bossed the game from the middle of the park – while Luke Ayling tormented Palace with his tireless running up and down the right wing. These three players would celebrate their 30th birthdays later in the year, and having spent their whole careers struggling to make it in the Championship, they now looked at home in a league they thought they'd never visit. It was an extraordinary transformation.

The same could be said about Gjanni Alioski, Mateusz Klich, Kalvin Phillips, Patrick Bamford and Jack Harrison, but I did wonder how the season might have panned out if Michaël Cuisance had passed his medical. If he had, there would have been no Raphinha, who brought the X-factor to a team that was otherwise workmanlike. On a freezing cold Monday night in West Yorkshire the Brazilian was on fire – what a shame nobody was in the ground to witness his masterclass – and Raphinha concocted the second goal with a darting run and venomous shot that the keeper could only palm into the path of Patrick Bamford, who tapped in the 100th goal of his career. There was another milestone in the Leeds team but Kalvin Phillips's 200th appearance ended in disappointment as he limped off the pitch in the final minutes, having battled on through injury until the points were safe.

This ninth victory of the season felt like a watershed moment. It wasn't as barnstorming as the win at Goodison and wasn't as impressive as the three points at Leicester, but it was an accomplished and comfortable Premier League success against an accomplished and comfortable Premier League side. It now felt like Leeds truly belonged, and they climbed into the top half of the table for the first time since the early weeks of the season, now just eight points behind fourth-placed Liverpool, with a game in hand too. These were dizzying heights, nosebleed territory for the younger fans; was it possible that Leeds could get back in the Champions League, 20 years since almost winning it? 'Right now we don't have the consistency to imagine being higher up the table.' El Loco's assessment was true, but it didn't stop me dreaming of 'living the dream' once again.

Arsenal 4 Leeds United 2

What better way to spend Valentine's Day than watching 11 polished turds teach 11 multi-millionaire 20-somethings how to really play football? Well, that was the plan, but on the morning of the game Kalvin Phillips was ruled out with injury, and without the Yorkshire Pirlo screening the defence, showing for every ball and launching attacks with his quarterback-style passing, I knew it was likely to be a very different story.

It didn't help that Robin Koch, the German international who was supposed to act as Phillips's understudy, had been injured for most of the season, and Pascal Struijk was again asked to step into the KP role, thus stepping out of the centre-back position he had excelled in to such an extent that the Netherlands and Belgium were vying for his allegiance at international level. Struijk had never looked as comfortable in midfield as he did in defence, and El Loco's selection drew derision from the Leeds Twitterati, who were convinced they knew better.

Bielsa would always admit his mistakes, but despite racing into a 3-0 deficit he did not blame his team selection for this defeat, nor would he blame the London Curse or his young goalkeeper, who conceded a poor goal at his near post after 13 minutes. He was then caught in possession and gave away a penalty, before being beaten at his near post again right on half-time. It was a horror show for the ice-cool Frenchman, one that Kiko Casilla would have been proud of, but it had been a dire first half all round – even worse than at Old Trafford, if not as painful.

The start of the second half brought no improvement. Hélder Costa had been introduced and was immediately caught in possession on the edge of his own box, resulting in a fourth goal for Arsenal and a hat-trick for their previously out-of-sorts star man, Pierre-Emerick Aubameyang. Only the post denied Aubameyang a fourth goal and Arsenal a fifth, and I wished the game to end there and then. Bielsa didn't, and with the home team relaxing Leeds worked themselves back into it. Struijk powered home a header from a corner, then Costa atoned for his earlier mistake by combining with the other half-time substitute, Tyler Roberts, to reduce the deficit to 4-2. There was still 20 minutes remaining when Patrick Bamford was sandwiched in the box by two clumsy defenders. It looked a certain penalty, but referee Stuart Attwell wasn't interested, neither was VAR, and thereafter Arsenal managed to stifle what had threatened to become a miraculous turnaround.

'The game was not over at 4-0, the game was over when Shackleton missed the chance in the 92nd minute.'

When analysing the match Bielsa was keen to have his team's second-half performance taken into account, but the focus from the mere mortals was on what went so horribly wrong in the first half, and the finger of blame was pointed squarely at the manager for his team selection.

On this day of love and romance I had spent most of my time in a blistering row with Lewis on WhatsApp – pre-match, through the match, and post-match. Lewis believed the line-up was a travesty from the moment it was announced, while I defended it even after the humbling defeat, because if Marcelo Bielsa didn't feel that Dallas, Klich, Shackleton or anyone else can play in Phillips's role, who were we to argue?

Wolverhampton Wanderers 1 Leeds United 0

As it happened, Marcelo Bielsa agreed with Lewis and the rest of the Leeds fans, and for the trip to Molineux he restored Struijk to his natural position alongside Cooper, with Ayling back in the right-back slot. Jamie Shackleton was given the nod to deputise for Kalvin Phillips, who wasn't only suffering from a muscle strain, he was now mourning the loss of his beloved grandmother too. Granny Val was an absolute treasure who stole a place in our hearts on *Take Us Home*, the documentary which serialised Leeds's rise to promotion under Bielsa. She seemed just like my nanna: salt of the earth, a heart of gold, and Leeds born and bred. Phillips was very close to his granny, who had raised him along with his mother, and what a wonderful job they had done.

By now the New Normal was so normalised that it didn't feel abnormal to be watching a Friday night match alone in the kitchen. On realising this I insisted Frankie watched the game with me, and after swift negotiations we decided she would watch the first half from behind her magazines, then go to bed at half-time. Frankie's input was to slag off Stuart Dallas for a slightly wayward back-pass, and to slag off Wolves for continuing to take short goal kicks when the defender would just boot it upfield anyway. Still, it was a lot better than arguing on WhatsApp.

Not that there was anything to argue about tonight with Leeds back to their normal selves, pressing aggressively and playing instinctively. They didn't dominate the match, but the defence was equal to everything Wolves had to offer and Meslier responded to his worst ever showing last time out with a string of solid saves. In fact, this match could be summarised as a tale of two keepers: one desperately unlucky, the other very lucky.

In the first half Mateusz Klich's clever shot from a tight angle hit the post and ricocheted off Wolves goalkeeper Rui Patrício's legs to safety, and in the second half Adama Traoré's rasping long-range drive hit the bar, ricocheted off Meslier's head, and rolled into the back of the net. To make matters worse, seconds before the goal Liam Cooper had missed the second of a hat-trick of glorious chances from the wicked dead-ball deliveries of Raphinha, heading straight at the keeper each time. And even more annoying, the free kick that led to Cooper's chance came from a deliberate handball by Conor Coady that prevented Bamford sprinting clean through on goal. Leeds didn't make a song and dance about it, so Coady wasn't even booked for his red card offence. Where is VAR when you need it?

VAR is always there when Leeds's opponents need it, and Bamford's blistering equaliser was chalked off for the tightest of offsides. Again, the lines drawn at Stockley Park looked very suspicious, leading to a funny meme on Twitter that portrayed VAR as a mass forensic investigation when Leeds score, and Chief Wiggum from *The Simpsons* eating a donut when Leeds concede. An infuriating exhibition of time-wasting by Wolves ensured there was only one more chance to equalise, and it fell to Hélder Costa, 12 yards out with the ball at his feet and 94 minutes on the clock. This could have been the moment Costa showed his former employers they were wrong to cast him aside; instead he justified their decision with a pitiful finish straight at Rui Patrício, who was named man of the match even though he'd have done well to get out of the way of the shots he'd saved.

Wolves had become the first team to do the double over Bielsa in the Premier League, but instead of delivering a barrage of complaints about VAR, and excuses about injuries and misfortune, in his post-match interview El Loco yet again displayed the integrity his peers so dearly lacked, 'It is our job to make sure luck is not a factor.'

Leeds United 3 Southampton 0

Having been leapfrogged in the table by Arsenal and Wolves in consecutive matches, Leeds were hoping to avoid an unwanted hat-trick as they prepared for a 12th vs 13th battle at Elland Road. Despite the successive defeats there was plenty to be excited about, starting with Bielsa's pre-match presser in which he declared his love of managing Leeds United, telling the world there was no better club to be in charge of, 'I go from day to day thinking I'm going to be here for the rest of my life.'

Hearing The Great Man talk like this melted my heart. I still couldn't believe he was ours.

Even more exciting was the release of prime minister Boris Johnson's roadmap back to the Old Normal. The UK's vaccination programme was well under way and the target was to have all Covid restrictions removed by 21 June, though the big news was the planned re-opening of football stadiums on 17 May, albeit at quarter-capacity. A quick check of the fixtures confirmed that Leeds's last match of the season was at Elland Road on 21 May; amazing news! With a maximum attendance of 9,600, half of the season ticket holders would miss out, but I was thrilled to have the prospect of returning to Elland Road this season when all had looked lost.

Perhaps the most exciting news of all (on a personal level) was an esteemed publisher agreeing to issue *Marcelo Bielsa vs The Damned United*, my account of Bielsa's first two seasons at Elland Road This was mind-blowing for me. I didn't even know I could write before Bielsa's extraordinary awakening of Leeds United inspired me to try, but the deadline for submission was approaching and I felt under immense pressure to perfect it. Every read-through brought 100 improvements, and my day job wasn't helping with the workload either. I had a massive proposal to submit on the same day as the book, so when the Southampton match rolled around at 6pm on Tuesday I was just too busy to watch it. Instead, I recorded the game, switched off my phone and locked myself in my office, finalising my work proposal so I could take Wednesday off to finish my book.

By 9.30pm my work was complete and so too was the Leeds game. Bielsa and the players were leaving a deserted

Elland Road and the Twitterati were flooding timelines with doom or delight, while I sat in my office none the wiser. All I knew was the team news, that Llorente had recovered from his third injury to make his third Leeds appearance in place of the unfortunate Jamie Shackleton, who was now injured himself. I also knew it was about time Leeds won without Kalvin Phillips in the team, and win they did, thanks to a wonderful second-half performance.

One of the main frustrations of watching on TV was the producer's insistence on showing multiple replays while play was ongoing. Being forced to watch a second replay of a nothing foul while you could hear the Whites zipping the ball about had me tearing my hair out, and the speed of Leeds's attack almost led to the cameras missing the opening goal of this game. Only on the replay (ironically) did we see Llorente's lovely sweeping ball into midfield and Roberts's sharp turn and slide-rule pass to split the Southampton defence. We did see Bamford's pinpoint finish, and the red-hot striker was up to third in the goalscoring charts, only behind penalty kings Mo Salah and Bruno Fernandes. The second goal was a piece of magic from Stuart Dallas. Was there any limit to this man's improvement? Receiving the ball on the edge of the box, Dallas drove forward and swerved a brilliant toe-poke away from the keeper into the bottom corner. Andy Hinchcliffe described it as 'not the most elegant finish of his career', but for me it was the exact opposite.

All season the media had droned on about Leeds burning out due to their extreme intensity levels, but the fittest team in the league showed no signs of doing that as they overpowered their ailing opponents, led by the wizardly wing play of Raphinha. His first touch was a marvel – every touch was a marvel – and the Elland Road crowd would have been lapping it up, 'RAPHINHA-A-A, RAPHINHA-A-A!' The Brazilian fittingly delivered the icing on the cake by curling a free kick low into the bottom corner, the goal his man-of-the-match display deserved.

It was such a shame for the Leeds fans to miss out on such a fantastic performance from their team, and for their team to miss out on the adulation that would have been showered upon them; nevertheless, on this occasion my feelings of regret were tempered by the relief of having such a tremendous season to help us through the lockdown. I could barely imagine enduring the pandemic with Leeds still rudderless, languishing in the lower reaches of the Championship. Gracias Marcelo!

Leeds United 0 Aston Villa 1

Dreadful. This was a dreadful match and a dreadful performance, on a dreadful pitch against a dreadful team and a dreadful referee. Leeds's first attack of the match was impressive – a quick, slick interchange that had Bamford attacking the box – but it was all downhill from there. The absurdly slippy new pitch took Bamford's standing leg, ruining his shot, and the miscued effort turned into a great cross that Raphinha was inches away from getting on the end of. A minute later, Villa's first attack suffered a similar fate with one significant difference. When Ollie Watkins slipped as he shot from outside the box, the ball went straight to his team-mate Anwar El Ghazi, who fired past Meslier to open the scoring. Typical!

For the rest of the match Leeds did not play well. Struijk was back in the defensive midfield role and struggled, Roberts was still in the attacking midfield role and struggled, Costa was given a rare chance ahead of Harrison and struggled, Hernández was introduced and struggled, and without any quality service Bamford struggled too. And then there was the pitch, which we were told was a grass and synthetic fibre hybrid, but it played like an ice rink, with players slipping on it left, right and centre, and mostly the ones dressed in white.

A slippy surface doesn't really affect you when you're only focused on incessant time-wasting and diving, and the referee gleefully lapped up Aston Villa's 'gamesmanship'. With all the predictability of Tyrone Mings heading clear every cross unchallenged, the official blew his whistle every time a Villa defender hit the deck, usually unchallenged. In the final seconds Bamford was grappled to the floor as he attacked a corner, but the referee, linesman and VAR all turned a blind eye, instead stopping the game because man mountain Mings had dropped to the floor with mysterious leg and head injuries. It was the final insult and summed up the game, while intensifying my hatred of referees, Aston Villa and modern football.

March 2021

Bryn Law – 'Down the years I had talked to many new players and coaches about the need to be aware of the pressure and expectation on every single game at Leeds United, and that's where Bielsa's genius lay. People can become overwhelmed by the pressure of the fans and make decisions on that basis, but Bielsa was above all that, it meant nothing to him, and he kept everything below him under control on that basis. You have to be focused and single-minded, and convince everyone else that you know what you're doing, and Bielsa would determinably plough that furrow that he'd created.'

6.	Liverpool	43
7.	Everton	43
8.	Aston Villa	40
9.	Tottenham	39
10.	Arsenal	37
11.	LEEDS	35

West Ham United 2 Leeds United 0

It was *Monday Night Football* duty again for Leeds, and their first trip to a stadium that could have been immortalised by the London Olympics but instead became a football ground everybody hates. Above all, it was the changing of its name to the London Stadium that annoyed me the most, stripping it of its heritage as if removing the word 'Olympic' would make everyone forget that the place isn't fit for football. What a shame for the West Ham fans who had lost their spiritual home for ever, although David Moyes's unlikely charge for Champions League football offered a chance to kick-start the revolution they were promised a 60,000-seater stadium would bring.

My respect for the law of averages had led me to predict victories in all the London fixtures this season, and with Kalvin Phillips back in the team I was confident the London Curse would finally be broken. How silly of me. The law of averages was no match for the London Curse. With just four minutes on the clock Tyler Roberts scored from Costa's cut-back. The flag was up, but that meant nothing; over to you, VAR. The replay seemed to clearly show Costa was onside, but the line drawers at Stockley Park found Costa's knee to be a good couple of centimetres offside. I'm not sure if it was an optical illusion but it looked a barbaric conclusion. Moments later Leeds scored again, Roberts the provider this time, with Bamford cleverly turning home at the near post. However, the assistant referee's flag was up again, and VAR confirmed the ball was out of play by a good couple of centimetres when Roberts crossed. Ten minutes after that Luke Ayling clumsily gave away a penalty, which Jesse Lingard took and Meslier saved, but the ball kindly rebounded back to the Manchester United loanee who fired home at the second attempt. So, after 20 minutes Leeds had scored two goals and saved a penalty, but trailed 1-0. The London Curse at its cheekiest.

The rest of the first half was dominated by West Ham, who scored again after criminal marking at a corner and they should have had a carbon copy third, but the post saved further blushes. At half-time I was really downbeat. Defeats were so much harder to take when you'd spent nine days waiting for the game with nothing else to look forward to in life, sitting alone in your living room without the passion and humour of the Leeds fans in the background to cheer you up, and with three numpties in a van interrupting the flow of the game and disallowing your goals!

Thankfully the second half restored some of my will to live. Klich, Costa and Roberts were all replaced, and Leeds looked a much better team. Four great chances fell to Bamford and Raphinha, and if one had hit the net the outcome could have been very different, but by the time Rodrigo failed to bundle home from three yards the game was up. The London Curse had prevailed again.

There was praise for Leeds after the match from Hammers captain Declan Rice and manager David Moyes, who both spoke of their relief to come away with a fortuitous result. It was scant consolation. After four defeats in five games the fear of sliding into a relegation battle moved from the back of my mind to the front, especially with Chelsea up next and a trip to Fulham to follow. The Cottagers were the occupants of the last relegation spot and a mini revival had brought them to within nine points of United. They also played in London. With fixtures against Manchester City, Liverpool and Manchester United to come in April, the nerves were jangling. Now was not the time to get dragged into a race Leeds hadn't even flirted with all season.

Leeds United 0 Chelsea 0

When the fixture list was released it felt like somebody had been looking out for us, with the home games against Chelsea, Manchester United and Liverpool all at the back end of the season, giving us the maximum chance of greeting our three biggest rivals with full houses. Sadly, it wasn't to be, which cushioned the blow of Frank Lampard failing to hang on to his job long enough to receive a barrage of abuse on his return to the Elland Road dugout.

Lampard had been sacked after his team blew a gasket in beating Leeds, falling from the top of the league to mid-table within a month. His replacement, Thomas Tuchel, was considered the brightest young manager in world football and exposed Lampard's managerial frailties with an instant turnaround. A previously leaky defence had conceded only two goals in the German's 12 games in charge (one an own goal), and he was yet to taste defeat. Although I'd have liked Bielsa to have the chance to put one over on Lampard, it was a relief not to have the past dug up again; the boring Spygate quips and questions, and Lampard's arrogance thinly veiled as modesty. The Leeds–Chelsea rivalry deserves more than that, and now it had a great young mind vs the greatest mind, leading to a great battle on the pitch, which, incidentally, had its best game since joining from Spurs.

Bielsa's team selection was again under scrutiny as he persisted with Tyler Roberts in the attacking midfield role, despite Rodrigo's return to fitness. Roberts had shown few signs that he was good enough to excel in the Premier League but El Loco was sticking by him, and having been proved right with Alioski, Dallas, Harrison and Bamford in similar circumstances – by affording them the time they needed to develop into the players he knew they could be – that was good enough for me.

Roberts responded with a man-of-the-match performance, one that should have won Leeds the game. He opened the scoring but the goal was disallowed for offside, and a little later he was denied by the faintest of flicks from the goalkeeper's middle finger, just enough to divert an expert chip on to the underside of the crossbar. It was as fractional as any VAR offside all season. In the second half Roberts had a new partner in attack as Rodrigo replaced the unfortunate Bamford, whose afternoon was cut short by injury with England manager Gareth Southgate in attendance and an international call-up within his grasp. Still, Roberts remained the major threat, and he created Leeds's best chance of the game but Raphinha couldn't connect cleanly enough to beat goalkeeper Mendy from eight yards.

It wasn't all about Roberts though. Chelsea had some decent players on the pitch too, but none of Kai Havertz, Hakim Ziyech, Mason Mount or Christian Pulisic, nor substitutes Timo Werner and Callum Hudson-Odoi, could find a way through Bielsa's 13th centre-back partnership of the season. Diego Llorente's impeccable performance was his best in a white shirt, while Pascal Struijk continued to boost his profile with another assured display beside him. Another clean sheet added to Illan Meslier's Premier League record-breaking tally for a goalkeeper aged 21 or under, and he achieved it thanks to a world-class save when Havertz carved out Chelsea's only clear opening of the match. The Frenchman stood tall and trusted his reflexes, duly springing his right arm to palm a ferocious close-range drive over the bar.

A pulsating 0-0 draw was a fair result, and one that Leeds could be extremely proud of. They had gone toe-to-toe with one of the best teams in the world, who would end the season as European champions.

Fulham 1 Leeds United 2

You could say Leeds's London Curse began on 19 March 2015, the day after they visited Craven Cottage and won 3-0. Perhaps someone smashed a mirror in the dressing room because in the six years since, Leeds had played 29 matches in London, winning only one and losing 22. Under Marcelo Bielsa, Leeds had played 15 matches in the capital, yielding no wins and only two draws. On 19 March 2021 they returned to Craven Cottage looking to prevent the London Curse from stretching into a seventh year.

It had been a long and lonely winter but, with the UK's vaccination programme motoring on successfully, lockdown restrictions were about to ease and this was the last match I would have to watch alone in this season (unless a new strain of Covid emerged that couldn't be controlled by the vaccine). This was a great relief. Apart from missing being at the games, I was sick to death of watching on TV, listening to clueless pundits spouting the same old rubbish about Ayling once playing for Yeovil (so what?), Bamford's previous failures in the Premier League (he'd only started two Premier League matches before this season), and the bizarre assertion that Northern Ireland international Stuart Dallas, aka the 'Cookstown Cafu', was born and bred in Leeds.

For the last game of lockdown I arranged a 'watch-along' over the phone with Lewis, George and Rick, which left me wondering why on earth we hadn't done it sooner. We chatted, laughed and drank merrily (well not Lewis, he was 573 days into a drinking hiatus) as Leeds dominated from the off, making the game look exactly what it was – a good Premier League team against a Championship team struggling to punch above their weight.

Leeds still had VAR to contend with though, and for the fourth time this season they had a goal ruled out for offside when both feet were onside. Tyler Roberts's shoulder was the offending body part on this occasion, drifting an inch offside and consequently denying Luke Ayling his first Premier League goal. At least we got to see Ayling's magnificent mane unfurled again in a repeat of the famous 'air-guitar' celebration from the last match of the Old Normal. Leeds were not to be denied for long, however. Fulham were caught cold by a quick throw which Harrison drilled low into the box and Bamford drilled low into the net. Having narrowly missed out on an England call-up – all but ending his slim hopes of playing in the Euros – notching his 14th goal of the season was the perfect response by Bamford.

By half-time the scores were level after Leeds were again undone by a corner. Nobody had conceded more than the 15 goals United had yielded from set pieces this season, and their prodigious goalkeeper prevented that number from growing by adding two more incredible saves to his highlights reel. Nevertheless, I was not overly concerned. Leeds were a class above their opponents and I was confident that it would tell; it did so on the hour mark. The goal was scored by Raphinha and the assist went to Bamford, but Kalvin Phillips deserved all the credit having steamed in to steal the ball in midfield and set up the attack. Fulham huffed and puffed but the result never seemed in doubt, and when the final whistle blew Leeds had finally laid to rest the London Curse, and with it any lingering relegation fears. Hallelujah!

The next morning came the news that the Leeds United family had feared for several weeks – the death of a true club legend, Peter Lorimer. With nicknames such as 'Hotshot' and 'Lasher' it's no surprise that Lorimer was the club's all-time record goalscorer, with 238 goals from the right wing. He made his debut at just 15 years of age and clocked up over 700 appearances for the Whites by the time he retired aged 39, having won nearly everything in Don Revie's famous team. And he would have won everything had his unstoppable volley in the 1975 European Cup Final not been controversially disallowed.

Like many of his former colleagues, Lorimer spent his post-playing days in and around the club, not only as an ambassador and board member, but also as a co-commentator and pundit on Radio Leeds. Having lost his team-mates Jack Charlton, Trevor Cherry and Norman Hunter in the previous season, and Paul Madeley the season before, this was another harrowing loss for the 'Sons of Revie', and two more legends, Terry Cooper and Mick Bates, would pass away in the summer, aged 77 and 73 respectively. Tragically, of the ten youngsters that came through the ranks to star for a decade in Revie's all-conquering side, only three remained with us, but the legacy of these legends will continue to shape the philosophy of our club for ever more. A club that they made great.

Bryn Law – 'Peter was, like Norman Hunter, someone I got to know as a friend. He was often the sub called off the bench if Norm couldn't get to a game, and he was an excellent co-commentator; knowledgeable, enthusiastic, and always Leeds. Always Leeds. After I'd left Radio Leeds, he was one of my go-to guys when I had to come up with a guest to talk about Leeds for a Sky Sports News report. A quick call to confirm, then I'd head down to The Commercial and we'd find a quiet corner, the lunchtime drinkers at the bar, and we'd do an interview and then just sit and chat. He had a great, dry, typically Scottish sense of humour. Those Revie boys, they were a different breed. Football gods but great human beings. I count it as one of the privileges of my life that I got to know them.'

April 2021

Bryn Law – 'Working for LUTV, we're there on behalf of the club and almost feel part of the team, and in the behind-closed-doors games we were not only representing the club but the fans too. Tony Dorigo, a brilliant co-commentator, was fully invested in this idea and we effectively became the away end, with the epitome being Stuart Dallas's winning goal at Manchester City. Tony's squeals of delight ensured that, on one level at least, it sounded like it would if the Leeds fans had been in the ground.'

6.	Tottenham	48
7.	Liverpool	46
8.	Everton	46
9.	Arsenal	42
10.	Aston Villa	41
11.	LEEDS	39

Leeds United 2 Sheffield United 1

The last time Leeds beat Sheffield United at Elland Road brings me to the third and final mention of feeling the presence of God in a football stadium. It was September 2010, and a dull Yorkshire derby was heading for a 0-0 draw as we entered the last ten minutes, when from my usual spot at the top of the gangway between N11 and N10 I noticed Lewis coming up the stairs. I hadn't expected to see him; earlier in the day I'd heard the heartbreaking news that his sister had tragically died. He looked a lost soul, desperately upset, and when he reached me we embraced without saying a word. Just then, a roar went up. Leeds had scored but we continued to hug tightly, before loosening our grips just enough to acknowledge each other's wry, sorrowful, and knowing smiles. A goal from above to lighten the load, if only for that moment.

You assume pigs will never fly and hell will never freeze over, and never in a month of Sundays did I expect Marcelo Bielsa to come face to face with Paul Heckingbottom in a Premier League match; the thought seemed entirely impossible. Yet here we were. 'Hecky' was El Loco's predecessor at Elland Road and spoke of needing new players to bring an intensity that was missing, 'wit' ball and wi'out ball'. It was a comment that would age terribly, as Heckingbottom's last line-up as Leeds manager was basically Bielsa's team for the following season. Perhaps he was a little unfortunate that a messiah had stepped into his shoes, and now he'd stepped into a messiah's shoes, having taken over in the Bramall Lane dugout from Chris Wilder, the man who led Sheffield United from League One to the Premier League after a 25-year absence.

After finishing ninth in the 2019/20 season, 2020/21 had been an unmitigated disaster for the Blades. They lost 15 of their first 17 games – drawing the other two – but had at least managed to exceed Derby County's record low points haul of 11 (ELEVEN) by the time Wilder left his post. Heckingbottom's first game in charge was a 5-0 thrashing at Leicester, and in his second match at Elland Road his team were torn to pieces again. The Whites opened the scoring when some classy play from Llorente, some tenacity from Dallas, and some electric dribbling by Raphinha set up a tap-in for Jack Harrison, and I told my LUFC WhatsApp group, 'This could be ten.' Yet despite their domination Leeds couldn't add to their lead and, almost comically in the circumstances, the visitors equalised with their first meaningful attack, right on half-time.

Within minutes of the restart the natural order was restored thanks to Phil Jagielka's third goal for Leeds, despite never having played for them. The Whites continued to dominate but Bamford, Dallas, Raphinha, Rodrigo, Roberts, Harrison and Alioski all failed with chances to finish the game off, and as a result, the threat of a sucker punch hung in the air. And it very nearly came in the 88th minute when Sheffield United's £24m summer signing, Rhian Brewster, hit a thunderous long-range volley that Meslier could only watch as it swerved inches wide of the post. It would have been a spectacular way for the young striker to open his account for the club, but it wouldn't have been worth the wait. Brewster had been a signing that reflected the shambolic season Sheffield United had endured.

Funnily enough, since 1998 every Yorkshire team that had been promoted to the Premier League had survived their first season and been relegated in their second (Bradford, Hull twice, Huddersfield, and now Sheffield United) and having surpassed the almost metaphorical 40-point mark, Leeds were halfway to continuing the sequence. The only focus now was on keeping the chase for Europe alive, but with daunting fixtures against Manchester City, Liverpool and Manchester United to come, if the Whites were to still have a chance come the end of April we were in for one hell of a month.

Manchester City 1 Leeds United 2

Since the epic 1-1 draw with City in October, Pep Guardiola's team had found their stride and won 27 of their 28 games in pursuit of a historic quadruple. The league title was all but wrapped up (14 points clear with seven matches remaining), the League Cup Final and FA Cup semi-final were just around the corner, and this meeting with Leeds was sandwiched between a Champions League quarter-final with Borussia Dortmund. The first leg had been won 2-1 and among his pre-match eulogising over Marcelo Bielsa, Guardiola had commented that El Loco's Leeds were the 'absolute worst' team they could face between the Dortmund games, which I think he meant as a compliment.

The lockdown restrictions had now been eased, but this Saturday lunchtime fixture would not be spent in the garden with no more than six mates or two households of mates – the weather was too unpredictable to make such plans. So once again I was watching on my own, although with expectations of taking a thrashing I was never enthusiastic about making an event of the occasion.

City kicked off and for a few minutes Leeds never touched the ball, and they didn't see much more of it for the rest of the half. Yet the defence was organised and disciplined, and the pace of Raphinha and Costa was a constant threat on the counter-attack. This was not Bielsaball as we knew it; The Great Man had devised a specific game plan to stifle City, and that was as surprising as it was to see Leeds take the lead in the 42nd minute. The counter was sprung from the left and Costa fed Bamford, who teed up Stuart Dallas, arriving from midfield to drill a low finish in off the post.

It was a great time to score, but in the 45th minute Leeds were again on the rough end of a controversial VAR decision. Liam Cooper cleanly cleared the ball ahead of Gabriel Jesus, though it was a meaty challenge and by modern standards I wasn't surprised to see the referee award City a free kick and book our captain. However, I was dumbfounded when it became clear that VAR were reviewing the decision, and apoplectic when the referee was called over to the TV monitor to look at the replay for himself. Among my many complaints with VAR was the tendency to only show the referee one angle of an incident, and Andre Marriner was shown the view that made Cooper's challenge look worse, rather than the angle that made it look completely innocuous. Cooper duly received his marching orders, and my fury was amplified by the pundits who unanimously agreed with the decision. Cooper's kicking foot did connect with Jesus's knee on the follow-through, but it wasn't malicious or even dangerous. If the decision wasn't ludicrous then the laws of the game certainly were.

I spent half-time furiously ranting over WhatsApp about what a mockery the ruling bodies had made of the sport I loved, but I knew Bielsa wouldn't even have thought twice about the decision, only the solution. His solution was to withdraw Patrick Bamford, surmising that two pacy wingers would provide a far more menacing outlet than the presence of a lone striker. But United's main focus was defending, and they defended their lead heroically until City finally picked the lock with 15 minutes remaining and equalised through Ferran Torres. Now it was all about hanging on for a fantastic draw, and the outnumbered visitors stood up to the challenge; tackling, harrying, heading and blocking, while an eerily composed Illan Meslier dealt with the myriad of shots raining down on his goal (29 by the final whistle).

'When Bielsa parks the bus he leaves the handbrake off,' somebody cleverly commented on Twitter afterwards, and as the game entered three minutes of added time, Meslier ended another City attack but did not sink to the floor and waste as much time as possible. Instead, he spotted Alioski in space and quickly threw him the ball. Instead of hoofing it as close to the corner flag as he could, Alioski played a one-two with Costa and looked up to see Stuart Dallas steaming through midfield. Dallas had put in a superhuman effort over 90 minutes but still had the energy to make a pitch-length sprint (with the confidence that he could make it back if possession was lost), and his endeavour was rewarded as the outside of Alioski's left boot provided him with a perfect through ball. Dallas held off the challenge of John Stones and calmly slotted his shot through Ederson's legs, and I watched in disbelief as the ball rolled towards the goal, then yelped for joy as it hit the back of the net. Ten-man Leeds were going to win at the Etihad! I was so elated at this mind-blowing goal that I celebrated with reckless abandon, although when Frankie burst into the room and semi-sarcastically asked if the goal had been VAR-verified, panic shot through me. Thankfully, the replay confirmed that the goal would stand and the ten men saw out the last two minutes to claim a famous and sensational result.

Bielsa had overcome Guardiola for the first time in his career, and I had never seen him happier. He laughed away while delivering a fittingly 'Loco' analysis, with his wonky glasses (apparently broken on the training ground by a wayward Bamford shot) enhancing the most heart-warming scene, 'This sounds strange to say; it would have been fair if City had won, but we deserved to win. The reason we deserved to win was because of the belief of the players, the character, the personality, the effort, and the fortitude.'

I was thrilled for the players and of course our beloved manager, but happier still for the thousands of Leeds fans who were 25 and under, who had never seen the Whites as a Premier League club, let alone seen them competing with and beating the best teams in the country. Personally, I was a little uncomfortable with raving over beating Manchester City, but the fact City weren't a great team in my youth was irrelevant. For the past decade they had been the best team, and one of the richest and most powerful clubs in the world, and Bielsa had beaten them in their own back yard with just ten men! It was arguably the best Premier League victory in the club's history.

Leeds 1 Liverpool 1

Leeds vs Liverpool on *Monday Night Football* instantly brings back memories of Tony Yeboah's iconic volley in 1995, the greatest goal I've ever seen live, but Yeboah got no airtime tonight. Nor did José Mourinho, who had just been sacked by Tottenham only six days before the League Cup Final. Even tonight's match got no airtime because there were far greater issues at stake. Football had been rocked to it's core by the news that 12 clubs had signed up to a European Super League, and this was not the power play from earlier in the season, nor the type of idle talk that had emerged sporadically at various times over the last 20 years. This was the real deal.

The 'Dirty Dozen' were Real Madrid, Barcelona and Atlético Madrid from Spain, AC Milan, Inter Milan and Juventus from Italy, and the Rich Six from England: Arsenal (currently ninth in the Premier League), Chelsea (currently fifth), Liverpool (currently sixth), Tottenham (currently seventh) and the Manchester clubs. These founders would be lifetime members of the Super League, a competition that would effectively replace the Champions League, though its existence would render the domestic leagues irrelevant for these participating clubs. The chairman of the ESL was Real Madrid president Florentino Pérez, who claimed the competition would 'save' football, but with his next sentence he confirmed the truth that everybody knew, that it was all about money: 'The only way of making money is by making more competitive games that are more attractive, that fans around the world can see.' Backed by American bank JP Morgan, the ESL would instantly clear the rising debts of all these ailing giants – they were trying to save the business of football by killing the game of football.

The backlash to the ESL from the rest of the football world was emphatic. Fans, players, other clubs, pundits, journalists and football's governing bodies unanimously condemned it, and Leeds vs Liverpool was the first match to take place in Europe after the news broke. I was gutted we weren't able to attend this historic occasion, knowing that a packed Elland Road would have done the event every justice. Instead, there were just a few hundred protesters – mostly Leeds fans but also some Liverpool supporters too – armed with banners and chants of disapproval, and boos for the Liverpool team bus when it arrived. Leeds owner Andrea Radrizzani made his feelings known via Twitter, saying, 'The clubs are the fans and we (the owners) are the keepers of the club,' and during their warm-up the Leeds players wore T-shirts proclaiming, 'Football is for the fans.'

In the backdrop of all this the match itself was practically deemed irrelevant, which is a real shame as it was one that Marcelo Bielsa described as 'beautiful', although Leeds, minus Raphinha who was ruled out with a dead leg, weren't at the races in the first half. With their backs against the wall the defence held firm, with one exception when Trent Alexander-Arnold burst through and squared for Sadio Mané, who tapped into the empty net. All eyes turned to VAR, but there was no knee hair, shoulder or big toe to come to Leeds's rescue and Liverpool had the half-time lead they fully deserved.

I headed to The Cricketers at half-time to meet Huddersfield Bill for a pint and a catch-up in the beer garden (as dictated by Covid restrictions; it really wasn't beer garden weather), while watching what I expected to be a low-key second half and a comfortable victory for Liverpool. It was the total opposite. Leeds came out all guns blazing and set up camp in Liverpool territory, with the champions restricted to just 29 per cent of the possession after the break.

Chances flowed regularly but Alisson in the Liverpool goal was looking unbeatable, and when Bamford lobbed the Brazilian but saw the ball cannon off the crossbar it just wasn't looking like Leeds's night. However, Lady Luck shined on United when Mo Salah dragged a clear chance to wrap up the points wide of the post, and a richly deserved equaliser finally arrived from an 87th-minute corner, with Diego Llorente the deserving scorer. When the beer garden erupted it was the first time I'd heard the roar of a crowd for almost six months, and it was a joy to experience on so many levels. I was thrilled for Leeds, thrilled for Llorente, and thrilled to give one of the 'dirty dozen' European Super League clubs a slap in the chops.

Another impressive point had been achieved against the elite, and the result kept Bielsa's boys in the hunt for European qualification. Actually, Champions League qualification was practically in the bag for Leeds if the ESL did go ahead. That was an exciting thought, but wholly overshadowed by the prospect of having just watched the last ever match between Leeds United and Liverpool. In his post-match interview El Loco gave his thoughts on the European Super League, which were as concise as always: 'The fundamental problem is the rich aspire to be more rich without considering the rest. What gives health to football is the possibility of the development of the weak, not the excess growth of the strong.'

In Jürgen Klopp's post-match interview he deflected the conversation, instead ranting about the Leeds fans who booed the team bus and the club's decision to lay out the anti-ESL T-shirts in the Liverpool dressing room. It was at this point that I started to believe the ESL was actually going to happen, but the following day Pep Guardiola passionately condemned the idea for its lack of competitiveness. It was the first chink in the ESL's armour, and later that evening a mass protest outside Stamford Bridge prevented the Chelsea team bus from entering the stadium until news came through that the Blues were pulling out of the European Super League, which sent the protesting fans into rapturous celebrations. It was the beginning of the end, and within 24 hours the ESL was cancelled. Football had won; it still belonged to the fans after all. Sort of.

Leeds United 0 Manchester United 0

This was the big one, the fixture we had missed the most through 16 years spent in the wilderness, and with lockdown restrictions eased I headed to Terry's to watch in his garden with the other McTague brothers, plus Barker, Rick and Joe. I should have been frothing at the mouth over the prospect of Leeds's first Premier League victory over the arch-enemy for 19 years, but amid the disappointment of an empty Elland Road the match felt a bit of a non-event, even before it was suffocated by a spineless referee, a resilient Leeds defence, and a depleted Leeds attack.

The referee deserves the first mention because he was here, there and everywhere, awarding every free kick the visiting players or technical area demanded. Leeds weren't allowed to be aggressive or win the ball but Kalvin Phillips still found a way; he was immense, and man-marked the dangerman Bruno Fernandes out of the game. Behind Phillips was a centre-back partnership that was starting to look like the first choice. Diego Llorente and Pascal Struijk were the backup options at the start of the season but they had been excelling for weeks on end, even against the best attacks the Premier League had to offer. Going forward though, Leeds offered next to nothing. There was a big penalty shout for a handball by Luke Shaw and a deflected Costa drive that arched agonisingly on to the roof of the net, but that was as close as Leeds could come without the injured Rodrigo and Raphinha to pull the strings.

And so the game ended in a drab goalless draw, and Leeds were now six unbeaten in a run that included games against two Champions League semi-finalists, a Europa League semi-finalist, and the reigning champions of England. In those four games Leeds had conceded just two goals, making a mockery of the early season claims that El Loco prioritised entertainment over results, that his tactics were naive and suicidal, and his players would soon burn out under such rigorous workloads. On the contrary; Bielsa and his players were learning, adapting and improving, and they had found consistency at the business end of the season. And with Manchester City defeating Spurs in the League Cup Final, it was now confirmed that finishing seventh would guarantee European qualification. The race was on!

May 2021

Bryn Law – 'It was emotional welcoming the fans back. So much had happened since that pre-lockdown game against Huddersfield Town, and the West Brom game was the first time anybody had the chance to acknowledge Leeds United's achievements. People were celebrating winning the Championship on the final game of the following season, it was just the maddest of situations.'

6.	Liverpool	54
7.	Tottenham	53
8.	Everton	52
9.	LEEDS	47
10.	Arsenal	46
11.	Aston Villa	45

Brighton & Hove Albion 2 Leeds United 0

When analysing Leeds's remaining five fixtures there was no reason to think El Loco couldn't lead them back into Europe at the first time of asking. Brighton, Southampton, Burnley and West Brom were all languishing at the bottom end of the table with their fates practically sealed, and the other match was against Spurs at Elland Road, presenting a chance to win a vital six-pointer against the team currently in seventh, who were a club in disarray. You couldn't have hand-picked the run-in any better.

That said, all the ingredients were in place for Leeds to lose at Brighton. Firstly, having gone undefeated against the world's best, the 'Leeds, that' effect suggested the Whites would crumble against relegation battlers. Secondly, Leeds had a terrible record against Brighton and had never even scored a goal there in the top flight. Thirdly, and most significantly, there was no Kalvin Phillips, and without the Yorkshire Pirlo United's win percentage during the season dropped from 50 to 25.

And so it transpired. Leeds put in their most limp performance of the camaign, only rivalled by the 1-0 defeat at home to the same opponents. From 60 per cent possession they didn't manage a single shot on target – they barely managed a shot at all – and in the end a 2-0 defeat was flattering, with the home side missing numerous glaring opportunities to turn a comfortable victory into an emphatic one.

It was an afternoon that summarised my worst fears for the season, that Leeds wouldn't have the quality to break Premier League teams down and wouldn't be tight enough at the back to keep them out. As such, this terrible performance served as a reminder of how brilliantly they had done. This was perhaps Leeds's 'normal' level – the expected level of promoted sides – yet The Great Man's magic touch had taken them almost to the brink of Europe.

Leeds United 3 Tottenham Hotspur 1

Despite the dismal Brighton defeat, Marcelo Bielsa named an unchanged team, challenging and trusting his players to bounce back against Spurs. With Rodrigo and

Raphinha on the bench, and Pablo Hernández frozen out entirely, Bielsa was relying on an attacking unit that, in the Championship, had barely mustered a goal without Hernández there to pull the strings. This game showed how much his team had grown.

From the first whistle Leeds were buzzing around Spurs, snapping at their heels incessantly. They were first to every loose ball, won every 50-50, and were vibrant in possession. Tottenham's World Cup-winning goalkeeper, Hugo Lloris, had already been forced into two great saves before Stuart Dallas hammered the ball into the roof of his net from close range, giving the Whites a lead they thoroughly deserved. It would be inaccurate to say the goal sparked Tottenham into life, but they did equalise soon after thanks to Son Heung-min's clinical finish, and soon after that the Leeds defence was breached again, though Harry Kane's clinical finish was ruled out when only his big toenail could have been offside. It was another farcical VAR decision that made a laughing stock of the sport; mind you, it was refreshing to see Leeds on the right side of one at last.

After sacking José Mourinho, Daniel Levy had appointed 29-year-old Ryan Mason as his temporary replacement, making him the youngest manager in Premier League history. A narrow defeat in the League Cup Final to Manchester City was no disgrace for Mason's managerial bow, and Spurs came into this game on the back of successive league victories that had rekindled hopes of Champions League qualification. Yet their players weren't up for the fight at Elland Road and it was no surprise that Leeds regained the lead before half-time, when the Alioski–Harrison partnership set up a tap-in for Bamford, his easiest goal of the season.

In the second half Leeds had some defending to do, and they did it faultlessly against a fearsome attacking unit of Kane, Son, Dele Alli and Gareth Bale, a quartet that must have earned almost thrice what United's whole squad was paid. Despite facing plenty of pressure Leeds always remained dangerous, and they put the game to bed in the 84th minute when Raphinha took Koch's defence-splitting pass perfectly in his stride, strode into the box and squared for fellow substitute Rodrigo to dispatch comfortably past Lloris.

Seeing the three summer signings combine like this, coupled with another tremendous Llorente performance, it was impossible not to wonder where Leeds might have been had the new additions been fit for the majority of the season.

United had followed their worst performance of the campaign with their best, a result that rubber-stamped the fantastic achievement of going undefeated against the Rich Six at Elland Road, and conceding only two goals in the process. Naive tactics, my arse! Regardless of United's emphatically improved defence and sustained superhuman energy levels, there was no sign of remorse from the gutter pundits, though the respected analysts and journalists continued to be in awe of Marcelo Bielsa's team, and George Caulkin of The Athletic hit the nail on the head when describing Leeds's 'bludgeoning' of Tottenham, 'What a collective performance this was, what a unit Marcelo Bielsa has created and what a perfect embodiment of club and place. Through innovation he has restored Leeds to themselves; ferocious, in your face, don't give a toss, nothing else matters. And above all else, really bloody good.'

Burnley 0 Leeds United 4

The UK's battle with the Covid pandemic was looking as close to the end as it ever had, and with cases and deaths falling to all-time lows prime minister Boris Johnson confirmed the roadmap out of this nightmare would continue as planned, into step two from 17 May. This was the final confirmation that Leeds fans would finally see their team play Premier League football on the last day of the season, albeit against a Championship team, with West Brom's relegation now confirmed (Leeds, that).

To prevent the final day from being a dead rubber United needed to take maximum points from their last two away games. Such a sentence would have terrified me at the start of the season, but it excited me now. Leeds were six points off the European places with three games to go, and with Kalvin Phillips and Raphinha restored to the starting line-up, and only Robin Koch unavailable (plus 'forgotten man' Adam Forshaw, whose period on the sidelines would soon be counted in years rather than months) Leeds were practically at full-strength. Burnley, meanwhile, were now assured of a sixth consecutive Premier League season after recovering from their dismal start, but with Bailey Peacock-Farrell between the sticks I was so confident of victory I even checked the odds for Leeds winning, though I could never bring myself to jinx the Whites by backing them.

Peacock-Farrell was Bielsa's goalkeeper in the first half of his first season and didn't do a bad job, but shot-stopping was never his forte and the first meaningful shot today beat him with ease. It came from Mateusz Klich, who continued his resurgence in form by carrying the ball 50 yards before curling it into the bottom corner from the edge of the box. Coming in the 44th minute, it was a great time to score. On the other side of half-time Meslier made his customary vital contribution by superbly denying Matěj Vydra in a one-on-one, and soon afterwards Jack Harrison doubled the lead by diverting Alioski's shanked drive past Peacock-Farrell with a flick of his boot. It was a finish that was as clever as it was nonchalant.

In the lead-up to this match, club CEO Angus Kinnear predicted Rodrigo would be Leeds's player of the season in 2021/22, this despite the 30-year-old record signing having endured a difficult first campaign at the club. Injuries and Covid had denied him a proper run in the team, and Bamford's fantastic form had prevented him from playing in his natural position as a striker, but today he came on for Bamford and showed his class in a superb 30-minute cameo, sealing the win with his first sniff at goal. Rodrigo received Harrison's lovely pass with a lovely first touch that took two defenders out of the game, then produced a lovely finish, dinking the ball over the advancing Peacock-Farrell and into the net. As clever as it was nonchalant.

Rodrigo scored the fourth too, but this was a team goal, one of the highest calibre. Stuart Dallas won the ball high in Burnley territory, and a dozen passes later Luke Ayling had it on the edge of his own box and chipped it into the centre of midfield, where Klich had run into space and chested into Kalvin Phillips's path. The Yorkshire Pirlo pinged the ball on the half-volley, a pass the Italian Pirlo would have been proud of, swerving low and hard out to Jack Harrison on the left wing. Harrison's touch was as perfect as the pass, and he didn't need to break stride before splitting the defence with a perfect through ball. It was a shame it wasn't Patrick Bamford sent clean through to complete the perfect goal for Bielsa's OGs (that means 'originals', for the non-millennials among you), but the fact it was a £27m Spain international that rounded the keeper and slotted into the empty net was another indication of how far these players had come. Before El Loco wielded his magic, Dallas, Cooper and Phillips hadn't been good enough to nail their places in a poor Championship side, Klich hadn't been good enough for a poor Championship squad, Harrison had spent the second half of 2017/18 on the bench at Championship Middlesbrough, and one top-half Championship finish was the high point of Ayling's ten-year career.

The following day Tottenham beat Wolves to end Leeds's bid for European qualification (barring an improbable swing in goal difference) and although it was disappointing to have come so close and miss out, I wondered whether it would turn out to be a blessing in disguise. Without the distraction of European football, perhaps Leeds could accelerate ahead of West Ham and Leicester, and Arsenal, Tottenham and Manchester United, back into the Champions League! With Marcelo Bielsa at the helm it didn't seem out of the question. Nothing did.

Southampton 0 Leeds United 2

The behind-closed-doors era was over, God willing, and 8,000 permitted fans were the opposite of crammed into St Mary's for a Tuesday teatime kick-off (hopefully the last we'd see of those too). Before the game Marcelo Bielsa revealed that he'd sent Mateusz Klich and Robin Koch on their holidays a week early. Both were carrying minor niggles and Bielsa felt it would be better to let them rest ahead of the European Championship, rather than involving them in the last two Premier League games. It was a sensitive and sensible decision, but a real surprise to see El Loco taking his foot off the gas. European football may have been off the agenda but a top half-finish was within United's grasp, which would still represent a marvellous achievement.

The team selection brought more evidence that El Loco was not 100 per cent focused on taking maximum points from the remaining fixtures, with Kiko Casilla and Liam Cooper returning to the team in place of two youngsters in the form of their lives, Illan Meslier and Pascal Struijk. In Kiko's case it was unquestionably a sentimental decision, and the end-of-season vibes the manager was giving off seemed to transfer to the players. The Whites struggled to get going as Southampton flew out of the blocks, trying to impress their buoyant crowd, but the visitors were able to handle the pressure with relative ease.

By half-time it was still 0-0, and in spite of United's underwhelming performance I was content. Southampton had thrown everything they had to no avail, and I was convinced Leeds would pick them off as they tired in the second half. My optimism remained high despite Bielsa continuing to treat the game like a friendly, making a pre-planned double substitution. Off went Llorente and on came Struijk – only fair they play a half each to allow Cooper to return to the fold – and off went Kalvin Phillips, sacrificed so that Gaetano Berardi could make his Premier League debut. Berardi was an out-of-contract 31-year-old defender when he snapped his cruciate ligament in a dead rubber at the end of the promotion season, but Leeds had rewarded him with a new deal anyway and everyone at the club was thrilled to see the cult hero back in action.

The second half panned out just as I expected (it's amazing how easy football is to predict when you aren't blinded by pressure and pessimism), and from the moment Bamford poked Rodrigo's expert through ball between the keeper's legs the result was never in doubt. Leeds had dropped fewer points from a winning position than anyone in the league, and their 'naive' tactics and 'burnt out' players secured a tenth away win of the season, aided by an injury-time goal from Tyler Roberts. It was the young Welshman's first Premier League strike, and despite Bielsa's apparent relaxation of focus he greeted it with his most emphatic celebration of the season. The double-fisted downward slam had become trademark, and he delivered five of them while screaming 'GOAL!' He was clearly pleased for Roberts, a player he had stuck with through thick and thin, and I'm sure he was relieved that his sentimentality hadn't cost Leeds any points, but most significantly this goal guaranteed his team a top-half finish.

El Loco had been very careful not to reveal any specific targets through the season. Early on he had remarked, 'Being the fourth-worst team is not the target,' and later in the season he'd commented on his side's failure to secure themselves in the 'fifth to eighth positions'. Even if top eight was Bielsa's target, he could not have seen this season as a failure. That his team were breathing down the necks of clubs who were established at the top of English football, who had spent countless millions in the pursuit of success, was a remarkable feat. All hail Marcelo!

Leeds United 3 West Bromwich Albion 1

A weird and wonderful season had a fairy-tale ending for me. For years I had been screwed over by the ticket office's online application system, but all those frustrations were washed away the moment I received the email. 'We are delighted to inform you' was all I needed to read as I yelped for joy – I was one of the lucky ones, I had been allocated a golden ticket, I was going back to Elland Road!

I didn't realise how lucky I was until texting my mates, none of whom had been allocated a ticket. Nor had my dad but he wasn't bothered; Park Fisheries doesn't open on a Sunday. My good fortune put paid to my target of running a marathon by the time I next attended a Leeds game – I'd given up hope and given up training – but on the night before my return to Elland Road I registered for the Yorkshire Marathon to make amends. I may not have run a marathon, but at least I was now committed to doing one.

It was such a strange feeling to be getting ready for the match. The emotions were swirling around inside me and I didn't even know what they were. I was happy but I didn't feel happy. I wasn't nervous but I did feel nervous. Maybe it was a type of survivor's guilt, knowing that so many of the Leeds United family wouldn't be there to witness this momentous occasion, the day we had all been dreaming of for well over a year now. It was truly bittersweet. I parked at the top of Beeston Hill and headed to Elland Road with a can of Stella to take the edge off whatever it was I was feeling, and as I turned the corner off Sunnyview Gardens only the overgrown shrubbery blocked my view of the stadium. Part of me wanted to speed up and part wanted to slow down, so I did neither and in due course reached

126

the stairway down to heaven. There she was in all her glory, with new floodlights looming over the West Stand.

There were still 90 minutes to go until kick-off and I'd planned to do a full lap of the stadium to take it all in, but found myself desperate to get inside. So I bought a programme for the first time in 25 years (actually, my dad bought them back then; this might have been the first I'd ever bought) and headed into the Kop, up the stairs and straight to my season ticket seat. After 442 days away, I was finally home. The next few minutes were spent thinking of the goals we'd missed, playing them out in my mind's eye, trying to bring the moments to life. It was the previous season's matches that were dominating my thoughts, the matches we were robbed of as Pablo Hernández dragged his team-mates to promotion. Ah, Pablo. This was the day we would bid him and the lion-hearted heart-throb Gaetano Berardi an emotional farewell. As if it wasn't going to be emotional enough.

As the crowd began to grow the players finally emerged for their warm-up, with Elland Road cheering like a goal had been scored at the sight of their heroes. The Leeds squad were equally over-excited, practically sprinting on to the pitch, and a surreal experience continued during the warm-up as I did something I never thought I would do in my life – bring a cheer from the Kop! A wayward Kalvin Phillips practice shot flew into the gangway next to me and I pounced on the loose ball before anyone else could. I carried it down to the walkway to give me more space and booted it as hard as I could back to the pitch. You instantly know when you've connected well with a football and I caught this one perfectly. The trajectory wasn't perfect though; for a moment I thought the ball was going to catch the edge of the Kop roof, but it sailed successfully over to the lads to a lovely cheer from my companions. A stumble as I jogged back up the stairs brought me down to earth, though not quite literally. The announcement of the teams brought further cheers, with Hernández and Berardi both named in a starting 11 that paid homage to the job Bielsa had done at Elland Road. The back four and midfield three were all players he had inherited from Paul Heckingbottom, when Leeds were bottom of the Championship's form guide. Now they were top of the Premier League's form guide.

With only a few minutes until kick-off Elland Road was rocking (I'm sure 8,000 didn't sound like this in the JPT!). 'Champions of Europe' bellowed around the ground, with scarves waving everywhere you looked, until *that* intro started playing over the PA system. Those notes, played by goodness knows what instrument, stir up so many emotions. They form the beginning of the club anthem, a song that embodies the soul of Leeds United and welcomed Marcelo Bielsa's team on to the pitch. 'HERE WE GO WITH LEEDS UNITED,' the first line was sung with such passion that I have tears running down my face just recounting it. 'WE'RE GONNA GIVE THE BOYS A HAND,' about time too. 'STAND UP AND SING FOR LEEDS UNITED, THEY ARE THE GREATEST IN THE LAND.' They bloody were un'all, over the last 11 games. By the time the chorus kicked in I was a mess, I couldn't even get the words out. I only managed the first syllable of 'marching' but recovered in time for the all-important 'na, nana, na, na, na', which had become an endangered species through the Premier League exile.

The Happy Losers

Just missing the chestnuts

World-class set up for West Brom

Shearer celebration for Newcastle

Bielsa celebration for Leicester

Glum after Arsenal

Happy after City

Out of lockdown for Liverpool

Down in front!

Home

The Lads

Into 'em Leeds

The Boy from Brazil

GOOOOAAAALLL!

Farewell Swiss Prince

Post-match Pablo Party

Anfield is only Anfield when it's full

Private show at Elland Road

Shit ground no fans

The Jessica Ennis Stadium

The 'away fans' celebrate breaking the London Curse

Who knew these interviews happened simultaneously?

Let's all laugh at Pep

Can the last one to leave please turn out the lights

A full Elland Road

It had been such a strange day, but within ten seconds of kick-off everything felt completely back to normal. Liam Cooper shielded a ball out of play next to the corner flag in front of me and West Brom's number two hit the deck holding his face, rolling around like he'd been poleaxed. I don't think I've ever been more furious in my life. Seconds into this dead rubber, a game Leeds fans had waited over a year for – 17 years if we're talking about the wait to see Premier League football, and a lifetime for many – this ignoramus was trying to get our captain sent off for nothing! I steamed down the stairs screaming and shouting, waving my arms so ferociously that I nearly dislocated my shoulder. I wasn't alone. Another bloke was stood next to me doing the same thing, and amid my fit of rage I was able to appreciate how brilliant it was to be back, to be able to unleash hell on these cheating bastards in the flesh. Chants of 'WANKER! WANKER! WANKER!' rained down from the terraces; Elland Road was alive again!

Something not so great to experience in the flesh was VAR, which took only seven minutes to rear its ugly head when a sweeping move brought a tap-in for Harrison. I cheered, knowing it didn't mean it was a goal, and when the flag went up I waited, knowing it didn't mean it wasn't a goal. Only when play resumed could I be sure it had been ruled out, but it mattered not. Just ten minutes later, Raphinha's corner was headed in at the far post and this time my only doubt was who'd scored it, and for some reason I thought it might be Berardi. The South Stand was going potty but people weren't invading the pitch, so I wasn't surprised when the PA announced Rodrigo's name, his fourth goal in four games. It was a carnival atmosphere as Bielsa's team toyed with their opponents, and the second goal came courtesy of a poorly struck Kalvin Phillips free kick that bounced past the hapless goalkeeper. This was far too easy, and the Yorkshire Pirlo looked embarrassed that his first Premier League goal had arrived in such a manner.

In the second half it was more of the same. Leeds were so dominant it felt like they could score ten if they wanted to, but the only one who was really trying to score was Pablo Hernández, and his growing desperation suggested he only had a set amount of time to do so. Sadly, after 65 minutes his time was up. Time was up for Berardi too, who was first to leave the pitch after hugs from his team-mates. Berra epitomised everything the Leeds fans want from their players and had possibly even set a new standard; there may never be another quite like him.

There may never be another like Pablo either (even if there was one like him 30 years earlier), and the little Spaniard was reduced to tears as he left the Elland Road pitch for the last time. He wasn't the only one. Realising we would never again see the ball at El Mago's feet was enough to bring any Leeds supporter to tears, and I'll for ever be grateful that I was able to see him play one last time.

For the next ten minutes the whole stadium chanted Pablo's name on repeat, only stopping when Leeds were awarded a penalty for handball. Now comes the proof that Marcelo Bielsa isn't beyond criticism! I could always find ways to defend El Loco, but I couldn't understand the decision to take Pablo off when he did. This was a meaningless game, United were cruising to victory, and

Tyler Roberts had already played more football than he would have expected this season. The crowd deserved every last drop of Pablo, and had he been given just ten more minutes we would all have seen him score or miss one last penalty. Patrick Bamford capitalised on The Great Man's misjudgement by slotting home his 17th goal of a season that had been as remarkable for him as it had been for the team.

We hadn't quite had the perfect ending, but it would have done very nicely indeed if the ref had just blown on 90 minutes. Instead, the occasion was soured. It all started when Phillips let the ball run under his foot, presenting an easy chance to Robson-Kanu who finished past Casilla. This was only a slight annoyance, an irrelevant blot on a comfortable victory, but Phillips wasn't done yet. With seconds remaining he flew into a sliding challenge, attempting to end the season on a high. It was a brilliant crunching tackle that brought the final cheer from Elland Road, but the smiles were turned upside down by the sight of Phillips writhing on the floor in agony. He had suffered a reoccurrence of his shoulder injury from earlier in the season, and as he gingerly left the field it looked as though his place in England's Euro 2020 squad was up in smoke. I was devastated for him.

There was a lap of honour at the final whistle and the fans waved a final goodbye to Hernández and Berardi. Bielsa did not join in of course (why would he be deserving of acclaim when it was the players who had done all the hard work?) and nor did Phillips, who I presumed was inconsolable in the dressing room. It was a sad way to end a day of many contrasting emotions, but the joy of seeing the Class of '21 from inside Elland Road ultimately overpowered them all. As always, Marcelo's succinct analysis hit the nail on the head: 'It was an unforgettable game.'

The Class of '21

MARCELO BIELSA'S Leeds United had achieved the best points total by a promoted team for over 20 years, a tally that may never be beaten again, such is the ever-growing gap between the Premier League and the Championship. What's more, they did it in a style that would go down in history. They annihilated every other team in the running stats, with figures that were quite literally off the charts. They tackled more than anyone despite being near the top of the possession stats too, and they were the true entertainers of the division, facing the second-most shots while having the fifth-most themselves.

Bielsa achieved all this with predominantly the same players he inherited from Paul Heckingbottom. Of the 13 outfield players who appeared in at least half of Leeds's Premier League matches in 2020/21, eight were at the club when Bielsa arrived and ten had been in his very first matchday squad. Had Pontus Jansson, Samu Sáiz, Jack Clarke and Kemar Roofe fully bought into The Great Man's ethos, perhaps he would have achieved all this without making any changes at all!

Each year Bielsa had improved the players, taking them from Championship also-rans to promotion contenders, then from contenders to champions, and even within the Premier League season they had vastly improved from the first half to the second. Bielsa's Burnout Boys conceded half as many goals in the second half of the campaign as they did in the first half, and ended the season alongside Liverpool as the Premier League's two form teams.

El Loco had received an avalanche of plaudits, but I still felt his work was underrated. In truth, you would have to have been a part of the club to fully appreciate what he had achieved. A group of average Championship players had become one of the best Leeds United teams of all time.

Premier League table 2020/21

	Pld	W	D	L	F	A	Pts
Manchester City	38	27	5	6	83	32	86
Manchester United	38	21	11	6	73	44	74
Liverpool	38	20	9	9	68	42	69
Chelsea	38	19	10	9	58	36	67
Leicester City	38	20	6	12	68	50	66
West Ham United	38	19	8	11	62	47	65
Tottenham Hotspur	38	18	8	12	68	45	62
Arsenal	38	18	7	13	55	39	61
LEEDS UNITED	**38**	**18**	**5**	**15**	**62**	**54**	**59**
Everton	38	17	8	13	47	48	59
Aston Villa	38	16	7	15	55	46	55
Newcastle United	38	12	9	17	46	62	45
Wolverhampton Wanderers	38	12	9	17	36	52	45
Crystal Palace	38	12	8	18	41	66	44
Southampton	38	12	7	19	47	68	43
Brighton & Hove Albion	38	9	14	15	40	46	41
Burnley	38	10	9	19	33	55	39
Fulham	38	5	13	20	27	53	28
West Bromwich Albion	38	5	11	22	35	76	26
Sheffield United	38	7	2	29	20	63	23

Part Two:

2021/22 – The Return of the Fans, and the Curse of the Damned United

Pre-Season 2021/22

AFTER WAITING 16 years for promotion back to the Premier League, the Football Gods decreed that Leeds fans would have to wait one more year before we could see it in the flesh. Whether that really could 'only happen to Leeds United' we will never know, but the fact of the matter is it did only happen to Leeds United. As spectacular as it was, the 2020/21 season almost felt like a trial run – a TV show to get us through lockdown – but with restrictions lifted the behind-closed-doors era was expected to be a thing of the past. The fans were coming back, and 2021/22 would be *our* first season back in the big time.

CEO Angus Kinnear had previously explained how the club's strategy on their return to the Premier League was to invest heavily in the first summer, with just a tweak in the second. The plan had worked a treat so far, but a quiet summer window was never going to wash with a large section of the fanbase who wanted to see Leeds kick on and build on their ninth-placed finish, to strike while the iron was hot, while we still had Marcelo Bielsa. The Great Man was now 66 years old and wouldn't go on for ever, even if that was what he imagined.

It's not like there weren't players who needed replacing either, although Gaetano Berardi and Pablo Hernández had barely contributed in the first Premier League campaign. The same applied to young left-back Leif Davis and controversial goalkeeper Kiko Casilla, who both headed out on loan with options to buy – their days at Elland Road clearly numbered. Gjanni Alioski definitely needed replacing, and where Pablo followed his heart and moved back to his hometown club (CD Castellón, of the Spanish third division), Alioski followed his head and moved to Al-Ahli in Saudi Arabia, signing a nice fat contract that would set him up for life. You couldn't argue with either decision.

Within a day of Alioski's departure Victor Orta had replaced him with Junior Firpo, a £13m signing from Barcelona. Firpo's career had stalled in two years at the Camp Nou, but Leeds were convinced the 25-year-old could still develop into a world-class left-back under the guidance of Bielsa. Everybody expected Firpo to be an upgrade on Alioski, but filling the void left by the tunnel-shaking, ball girl-kissing, dolphin-screeching, stomach-biting Macedonian would be impossible. Alioski was one of a kind, an effervescent character and exactly the type of team-mate needed in the pressure-cooker of Leeds United, where he would always remain a hero.

It was no great surprise, and no great concern to me, that Firpo was the only major transfer of the summer. I had full faith in El Loco and his squad, and respected the board's strategy too, especially considering United's net spend ranked among the largest in world football since they were promoted back to the big time. The signing of Firpo, and a handful of youngsters for the development squad, along with the conversion of Jack Harrison's three-year loan deal from Manchester City, had taken the club's outlay in the last 12 months to around £130m, and this during a 'Covid year' too.

One deal that remained incomplete until the eve of the season was the small matter of Marcelo Bielsa's contract. He once again spent the summer as a free agent, and again nobody worried for a moment that he would be going anywhere, because El Loco literally went nowhere. He turned up at Thorp Arch every day to oversee improvements to the training ground, and paid out of his own pocket for a new gym to be built on site for himself and his staff. Bielsa wanted to ensure he was as fit and sharp as he could be for the new season; healthy body, healthy mind, and all that.

The highlight of summer 2021 was Euro 2020 (not a typo!), in which the breakout star was Leeds United's very own Kalvin Phillips. The Yorkshire Pirlo drew praise from legends of the game (from Xavi to Pirlo himself) for his high-octane performances in a more advanced role in England's midfield, and played more minutes than any other outfield player as England went all the way to the final before losing on penalties to Italy. My anxiety over the prospect of Kalvin stepping up and missing the vital kick made me worry for the wellbeing of his mother, but thankfully it was two Manchester United players who cost England their first European title.

The Euros helped the summer break pass quickly, but an outbreak of Covid following chaotic and riotous scenes at the Wembley final triggered grave fears of a trademark government U-turn on the decision to lift restrictions at football grounds. My fears were ill-founded. The plan for full houses across the country was going ahead, and with the vaccination roll-out almost complete I was hopeful this really could be the end of the nightmare pandemic. Masks were still required in some public places, but otherwise we were back to normal life at long last.

Leeds's first pre-season game was at Blackburn, ironically the last ground I was due to visit before football went behind closed doors almost 18 months earlier. Under Bielsa, friendlies had even less significance than for other teams; they really were just a continuation of pre-season training (later in pre-season Leeds would play two games in one day against Ajax, with some players appearing in both) and at Ewood Park the players played like they'd just completed a murderball session in the afternoon, and they probably had. Hence they struggled to a 1-1 draw, but the highlight was never going to be the football, it was all about being there, and shivers were sent down my spine as the players were serenaded by the 4,500 travelling fans, who had waited over a year to finally chant 'CHAMPIONS! CHAMPIONS! CHAMPIONS!' It really whetted my appetite for the new season, and Premier League football at a packed Elland Road. A whole new ball game!

August 2021

Bryn Law – 'It was a noticeably, significantly different season to the one that had gone before it. Whether it was personnel missing, or whether the system was beginning to show some of its flaws, there was a very different vibe in that second season in the Premier League.'

Manchester United 5 Leeds United 1

'Scum away'; what a way to kick off the new Premier League season! So good that you wonder whether it really was randomly generated, or decided by an algorithm that could calculate the fixture that would generate the most interest globally. Either way, I wasn't complaining. Playing the champions at Anfield was Bielsa's perfect curtain-raiser to life in the Premier League, and the War of the Roses was a spectacular way to welcome back the fans.

I had no idea what to expect at Old Trafford, but as I crossed The Stray en route to The Alex I could at least rest assured that Leeds couldn't possibly make a worse start than last season's 2-0 deficit in under three minutes. That said, the news that Kalvin Phillips was not yet Bielsa-fit, following an elongated break after the Euros, had me fearing the worst again. My concerns were eased on arrival at The Alex, where I found Paul and Barker sitting at the very table from which I watched Huddersfield send Leeds to the Premier League. That felt like a good sign. It also felt good to be able to go to the bar and order your own drinks, rather than relying on the attentiveness of the bar staff to keep the pints flowing. All Covid restrictions had now been lifted but the pub was nowhere near as busy as it would have been in the Old Normal, when it would have been ten-deep at the bar and good views of the telly would have been at a premium. You couldn't blame an early kick-off time – this was Leeds United v Manchester United! – and the lack of atmosphere, coupled with the realisation that two years of living in solitude had affected people's behaviours in such an extreme way, was somewhat deflating.

Once the match started it didn't matter what was around me, I may as well have been in the ground. Whenever Leeds attacked I couldn't stop myself screaming them on, and Leeds attacked a fair bit, looking well capable of hurting their opponents. But the orchestra was slightly out of tune and the little interchanges, big diagonals and final passes weren't quite coming off. At the other end there was no repeat of last season's flurry of early goals, but Leeds did look vulnerable. They survived for 30 minutes before being punished by Bruno Fernandes, who opened the scoring after wandering through the middle of the defence untracked, and at half-time I was happy to still be in the game. Leeds had been sloppy, but a second-half tweak could be all that was needed.

Bielsa duly replaced the ineffective Rodrigo with Junior Firpo, enabling Dallas to move from left-back into midfield, and four minutes later Dallas picked up possession in the middle of the park and laid the ball into Luke Ayling's path. Ayling took a touch and unleashed a thunderous strike, of which the camera had the perfect angle as the ball soared past a fully stretched David de Gea and into the top corner of the net, sending us into manic celebration. Leeds had equalised at Old Trafford with an absolute wonder goal, and to be able to celebrate by hugging strangers elevated the ecstasy. What a moment!

Our delight quickly turned to despair. Immediately after the equaliser, Paul Pogba received the ball in acres of space in midfield, played it into acres of space behind the defence, and Mason Greenwood clinically restored the lead. Two minutes later it was 3-1, six minutes after that it was 4-1, and as I sat in a state of shock – less than 20 minutes since the equaliser – Fred made it 5-1. Our worst nightmares were once again unfolding in front of us at Old Trafford, this time with 72,000 home fans to ram it down our throats.

Trailing 5-1 with 20 minutes remaining was actually an improvement on last season's 6-1 with 30 minutes remaining, and once again the final quarter brought no further disgrace. However, when I got home it all sunk in. I was furious Leeds had allowed themselves to be humiliated by the arch-enemy again, and the pain of suffering a repeat of 2020/21 was unbearable compared to last season's 'freak result'.

'There is a special moment in a team's development when the recognition of what happened before disappears, and the demand for what's next increases.' El Loco's words from the pre-match press conference were even more relevant afterwards. The players owed us big time for this.

Leeds United 2 Everton 2

By the eve of the Everton game I had swung 180 degrees. In his pre-match presser Bielsa spoke of the team's responsibility to 'pay the debt' to the fans for the suffering they had caused, but it was then I realised it was us who owed the debt. The fans owed their manager and his players patience and forgiveness, and acceptance that their exhilarating over-commitment to attacking cannot work every week. If it did, Leeds would be the greatest team in the history of football.

The magnitude of the Old Trafford defeat threatened to overshadow the Everton game, but I was certain the negativity of the previous week would totally evaporate on arrival at a packed-out Elland Road for the first time in 17 months, for the first Premier League home game in front of a packed-out Elland Road for 17 years. As it happened, the negativity evaporated on arrival at Park Fisheries for our ritual pre-match feed. We were amazed to see beautiful flowers and brand-new parasols that transformed the outdoor 'restaurant' from its previous squalor, and there was another pleasant surprise when the goods arrived in little cardboard boxes, along with generously sized, high-quality paper napkins. On the fish and chips themselves the verdict was unanimous; me, my dad, and my nephew Lucca all agreed they were undoubtedly the best ever, and just to top off the whole experience it started raining, with not a drop landing on any of us. Gone were the days of rushing to the bus shelter over the road in adverse weather conditions – this was a whole new ball game!

Gone too were the days of walking down Beeston Hill. My dad was worried his ageing legs wouldn't carry him back up it after the game, so we headed to the parking spot I had used during my dad's post-O'Leary exile, by the Matthew Murray site earmarked as the future home of Leeds United's training complex. It was a far less glamorous walk, but my dad was delighted with the minimal undulation.

Everything felt strangely normal as we approached and entered the Kop, but once in our seats we were greeted by luminous yellow flags for everyone to wave as the teams came out. This 'forced fun' made me nauseous but as kick-off approached Elland Road did look impressive, and sounded astonishing. As the players entered the pitch, 'Marching on Together' was sung so loudly that it completely drowned out the PA system, and I couldn't help but chuckle as both teams stood in a line, listening until the end as if it were the national anthem. The Everton players must have felt ridiculous, or in awe.

The game kicked off and the first chant went up immediately, one that was so Leeds, and so un-Premier League, 'GET INTO 'EM, FUCK 'EM UP!' The players didn't oblige and Everton registered their first shot at goal within ten seconds, then from the resulting goal kick Leeds swept forward, but Harrison and Firpo couldn't quite fashion a chance for Bamford in the centre. It was a rip-roaring start and the pace barely let up all game. There were just three occasions of respite: when Yerry Mina had an off-the-ball tickling contest with Bamford, when Richarlison pretended his head hurt, and when VAR took three minutes to award Everton a penalty for a tug by Cooper on Dominic Calvert-Lewin. The striker converted emphatically but Leeds responded in trademark fashion, levelling thanks to a swift and direct counter-attack that was calmly finished off by Klich. Elland Road erupted and once again it felt wonderful to reach down and bear hug the bloke below me (I still wasn't even hugging my own parents, just in case I infected them with asymptomatic transmission).

In the second half Everton regained the lead and had chances to extend it, while United struggled to reach anything like their scintillating best. Raphinha didn't though. The scowling Brazilian had the bit between his teeth all afternoon, and his face never altered even after producing a sensational equaliser from 20 yards, an explosion off his boot that bulged the net before you could even hope it would. Unfortunately, both Lucca and I thought we'd spotted an offside in the build-up which took the edge off our celebrations, and I was only able to acknowledge the goal once Everton actually kicked off. Bloody VAR, even ruining goals they don't disallow.

Our return to Elland Road almost had a fairy-tale ending as Leeds nearly stole a 3-2 win with the last kick of the game. The big chance fell to Harrison, but his scuffed finish presented a secondary chance to Bamford, whose goalbound effort was blocked by the outstretched boot of his old foe, Mina. The towering Colombian celebrating in Bamford's face at full time spoke volumes about how far Bamford and Leeds had come while the fans had been away. Mina had won a tough battle against one of the Premier League's top strikers, and his multi-million-pound team-mates and Champions League-winning manager (now Rafa Benítez, after Carlo Ancelotti had moved to Real Madrid) had earned a great point against one of the Premier League's top teams.

Although this was my second game back at Elland Road, I will always remember it as the day the Leeds fans returned. The West Brom game had practically been a testimonial compared to this intoxicating Premier League battle, and the buzz of experiencing Elland Road in 'bear pit mode' carried me through the whole of the next week. I hadn't realised how much I'd missed it, and had forgotten how much I loved it.

Burnley 1 Leeds United 1

In the lead-up to the Burnley game Patrick Bamford finally received the international call-up that had been tantalisingly close for months. Having turned down the Republic of Ireland's advances when he was a lambasted Championship striker, this was a victory for self-belief and another impressive notch in the career of Marcelo Bielsa. Since arriving at Leeds, El Loco had re-ignited the international careers of Mateusz Klich and Liam Cooper, turned Bamford into an England international, and Kalvin Phillips into England's player of the year! Phillips won the prestigious award having been the heartbeat of the side that almost won the European Championship, and the video of his midfield partner Declan Rice handing him the trophy was typically heart-warming, with Phillips as modest as ever, 'I got 40,000 votes? Leeds fans, that!'

The match at Burnley had been picked for *Super Sunday*, so once again it was over to The Alex and once again the pub was far from full, although at least I couldn't get a seat this time. Playing in the 3-3-1-3 formation they rarely excelled in, Leeds struggled to control a niggly first half, though they did stand up to the physical challenge, and the only time their goal was threatened was when Bamford diverted a corner against his own post. However, in the second half Leeds lost their way entirely and Burnley deservedly took the lead when Chris Wood prodded in a scrappy opening goal. There were still 30 minutes remaining but it felt like there was no way back for the out-of-sorts visitors, who increasingly sought out Raphinha in the hope he would conjure up a bit of magic. With four minutes remaining he did just that, bamboozling ex-Leeds left-back Charlie Taylor, who was left flat on his face as the Brazilian's cut-back was hit towards goal by Jamie Shackleton and deflected into the path of Bamford, who celebrated his England call-up by flicking the ball into an empty net.

The scruffiness of the goals was reflective of a low-quality battle, but having not drawn a single away match in the previous season I tried to see this as an indication of progress, that Leeds had avoided defeat while failing to find their rhythm. With the Whites still winless this flimsy theory wouldn't be enough to bring calm during the international break – only an expensive signing could appease the fanbase now, and the following day a two-and-a-half-year saga was finally completed with the signing of Dan James.

As a young winger at Swansea, James had been Bielsa's only target in his first January transfer window and Victor Orta duly delivered him. Well, he delivered him to Elland Road, but at the 11th hour (literally) Swansea pulled the plug and James returned home with his tail between his legs. Five months later he signed for Manchester United, but after two inconsistent years at Old Trafford the 23-year-old whippet was replaced by 36-year-old Cristiano Ronaldo, and Leeds pounced to capture the Welshman for £25m (almost £20m more than the fee they had previously agreed with Swansea).

To make way for James, Hélder Costa was sent on loan to Valencia, so completing Leeds's transfer window. It remained a tight-knit squad but I was more than happy, believing this was the way Bielsa kept the players to stick with his unrelenting training programme; the secret behind the phenomenal running stats that were key to Bielsaball. It felt like everything was in place for another fantastic season.

September 2021

Bryn Law – 'We were reminded why it was so important to have fans in the ground, the noise. This was the thing that had been missing, and it was a welcome trade-off for the extra hassle getting home! As a commentator you work off the atmosphere, we go on that journey with everybody else, and it inevitably lifts what you do to higher levels when there are 35,000 people in the ground.'

15.	LEEDS	2
16.	Burnley	1
17.	Newcastle	1
18.	Wolves	0
19.	Norwich	0
20.	Arsenal	0

Leeds United 0 Liverpool 3

With the Yorkshire Marathon just five weeks away my training was reaching its peak, and on Saturday morning I ran 28km. By Sunday afternoon my body was protesting furiously, and the walk to Elland Road was so painful that my dad almost outpaced me despite now being a self-diagnosed invalid. Once finally inside the ground the atmosphere was bubbling, reminiscent of a play-off or

European semi-final, and worthy of a famous old rivalry. Some generous cup draws had allowed Leeds to continue to lock horns with the big boys of English football throughout their wilderness years – Liverpool home and away, Manchester United home and away, Tottenham home twice, and away, Arsenal home, and away thrice, and Chelsea at home – but hatred seemed to be cast aside for these games, with the fans just grateful to face off with each other again. The heat of a Premier League clash restored the cutting edge, and I welled up as 'Marching on Together' greeted the players on to the pitch. How I'd missed this. Half my life had been wasted in the EFL.

In a blistering opening Leeds carved out a glorious chance for Rodrigo, but the misfiring forward fired woefully down the throat of Alisson in the Liverpool goal. The Reds weathered the early storm and took the lead in the 20th minute when Trent Alexander-Arnold raced to the byline and squared for Mo Salah to tap home. It looked far too easy, and only got easier for the visitors as they missed three gilt-edged chances in the next five minutes. Reaching the break just 1-0 behind felt like a win, but barely five minutes after the restart an incredible goal-saving tackle by Struijk was rendered irrelevant as Liverpool doubled their lead from the resulting corner.

The outlook was bleak but the Elland Road faithful still roared their team on, and the players responded in kind. Tyler Roberts had replaced Rodrigo at half-time and wasted two chances in quick succession, but on the hour mark an incident occurred that took the wind out of United's sails. Pascal Struijk dispossessed 18-year-old Harvey Elliott with a perfectly fair sliding tackle, but Elliott's leg got tangled in Struijk's trailing leg and the teenager's ankle was left badly dislocated. A lengthy stoppage ensued, during which a red card was brandished at Struijk, which seemed a bizarre decision considering the referee had initially waved play on, and an outrageous decision considering no VAR review had taken place. The referee's only consultation on the matter had been with Liverpool's manager, Jürgen Klopp, who had invaded the pitch to remonstrate with him while Elliott received treatment. Make of that what you will.

The ten men battled on admirably, and almost halved the deficit when a spectacular 50-yard lob by Bamford was tipped over by the back-pedalling Alisson, but despite a spirited effort the Whites only avoided an embarrassing scoreline because it took Sadio Mané ten attempts before he finally scored in injury time. Nevertheless, 'WE'RE LEEDS, AND WE'RE PROUD OF IT!' was a fitting last chant to bellow around Elland Road; neither players nor fans could have given more.

Newcastle United 1 Leeds United 1

When I saw on Twitter that tickets were available in the home end for the trip to Newcastle I jumped on it right away. It was a Friday night fixture and being at the game would be the only way I could avoid the temptation of breaking my alcohol ban ahead of the marathon, and if I did manage to resist the pub I'd be watching all alone in the kitchen, feeling sorry for myself. I'd done enough of that to last a lifetime, so I impulsively joined the Newcastle United supporters' club and bought a ticket as close to Bielsa as I could get.

The prospect of being 'close enough to smell Bielsa's bucket' pricked my dad's interest so I got him a ticket too, and having chauffeured me up and down the country through my teenage years, the circle of life decreed it was time I started returning the favour. I went above and beyond the call of duty by dropping the old man at the ground before finding a parking spot, and we met back up in the 'Wor' Jackie Milburn Stand (second cousin to the great Jack Charlton) 20 minutes ahead of kick-off. I'd been to St James' Park numerous times and had never liked it since the redevelopment work at the turn of the century, but that opinion was formed from high in the upper tier which dwarfed the rest of the ground. From our seats in the lower section, St James' Park was stunning.

Their stadium aside, Newcastle were a complete mess. The fans hated both the owner (Mike Ashley) and the manager (Steve Bruce), and they weren't too keen on the players either, who'd registered just one point so far this season. Leeds had troubles of their own though. Llorente had hobbled off against Liverpool, Koch was still struggling with a 'pubis' injury, and Struijk was suspended, having lost his appeal against his red card despite everybody – including the unfortunate Harvey Elliott, but excluding his manager – agreeing that it was a clean and fair tackle.

It was all change at the back but the attack remained unchanged, with the under-fire Rodrigo retaining his place despite a poor start to the season. Rodrigo answered his critics by orchestrating a tremendous first-half performance with Hernández-like dictatorship, and scored the opening goal without even touching the ball, as his clever dummy deceived the goalkeeper and allowed Raphinha's whipped cross to nestle in the corner of the net. Make no mistake, this was Rodrigo's goal, but while the streets would never forget, those pesky record books wouldn't even credit him with an assist. Only 13 minutes were on the clock but the goal broke the home fans' already thin patience. The Toon Army broke into a chorus of boos and chanted for the manager and the owner to go, while I sat there deadpan, trying to steal a glimpse at the celebrating Leeds fans through my best attempt at disdain-filled eyes.

At this point it felt like the Whites would run riot – they looked as far above Newcastle's level as Liverpool had looked above Leeds's – but when the home side started to get Allan Saint-Maximin on the ball the game changed. The Frenchman was too quick and powerful for the Leeds defence to stifle, and his trickery led to several chances that his team-mates couldn't convert. If Newcastle were going to score then Saint-Maximin would have to do it all himself, and he did so by dancing across the Leeds box and shooting low beyond the keeper. I stood and clapped politely, trying my best to mask my disdain-filled eyes.

The match was now swinging from end to end at breakneck speed, 'like a basketball match' as the pundits would often remark (so often it was becoming a cliché), and the last action of a breathless half brought a scintillating counter-attack that Junior Firpo launched terrifically but concluded terribly, by half-volleying over an open goal from six yards. My dad and I were in total agreement during our half-time debrief; we were in awe of the entertainment on show and, despite the frustration of not having the game wrapped up, we both felt lucky to be witnessing such a fantastic match.

But that was as good as it got. After the break Newcastle tightened up and Leeds lost their spark, and the game fizzled out into a disappointing 1-1 draw. With five matches played Leeds were still winless and panic was setting in online, but the game left me with a completely different feeling. Such was Leeds's commitment and entertainment value, I was able to enjoy the match even though the result didn't go our way. Perhaps that is the essence of Bielsaball, bringing pride and joy regardless of the result. That said, a win wouldn't go amiss.

Leeds United 1 West Ham United 2

In a moment of supreme generosity, for my brother-in-law's birthday I gave him my ticket for the West Ham game so he could join his son and my dad in the Kop. It was the greatest gift I could offer, but the gesture was double-edged. Not only had I saved myself the hassle of thinking of a present and paying for it, I was also going on a family trip to Wales and this way we wouldn't have to rush home, and I wouldn't have to rush off as soon as we got back, leaving Frankie holding the baby. Nevertheless, it was still a significant sacrifice, and it was gut-wrenching to drive directly past Elland Road on the way back from Llandudno, with Leeds fans jamming the other side of the road, excited for the game. Solace was found in Leeds's formidable record in home matches I had missed. The Whites always seemed to win when I was travelling with work and had won four of the five home games I'd missed during the Bielsa era (not including the behind-closed-doors matches), so I fully expected my absence to deliver the first win of the season.

I began to regret my decision during a pulsating first half. Leeds put in a superb display, taking the game to West Ham and deservedly scoring first despite missing (deep breath) Koch, Llorente, Struijk, Ayling, Harrison, Bamford and Forshaw. The goal was a beauty too, a typically rapid counter-attack that ended with Raphinha's cool and clinical finish into the bottom corner. The Brazilian had been at his brilliant best and was denied a near identical goal by the upright, while at the other end 19-year-old Charlie Cresswell was enjoying an excellent Premier League debut off the back of a starring role in the midweek League Cup tie with Fulham. Leeds had scraped through thanks to a dramatic 6-5 victory on penalties, and because of the lengthy injury list Bielsa was unable to freshen up his team for either match. In stark contrast, West Ham had made 11 changes for their 1-0 League Cup win at Old Trafford, and in the second half at Elland Road their fresher legs told. Leeds lost their verve and West Ham took control, yet they only levelled thanks to a wicked double deflection off Cooper and Firpo that left Meslier with no chance. Moments later Raphinha was withdrawn, and with that the home team's threat completely disappeared.

West Ham's powerhouse striker, Michail Antonio, was in the form of his life this season, averaging a goal a game. Today though, he had struggled to get the better of Leeds's teenage debutant and was lucky to still be on the pitch following elbows to Raphinha, Cooper and Meslier; the latter resulting in a disallowed goal and a bloodied mouth for the young French keeper. All those sins only earned Antonio a booking, and he capitalised in injury time by steaming through a stretched defence and finishing with the confidence of a man who could do no wrong in the eyes of his fans, manager, team-mate, or officials. What a bitter pill to swallow, especially as it plunged Bielsa's team into the relegation zone.

The players still received a rousing reception on their lap of Elland Road after the match but the response on social media wasn't quite as sympathetic, as supporters panicked at the winless start to the season. The reaction of the Twitterati was frustrating to read, as it always was, but El Loco's words provided the antidote, as they always did: 'The succession of bad results affect the morale of any team. When the performance is not negative, the recovery is more probable.'

October 2021

Bryn Law – 'Leeds United is a proper roller-coaster club, with huge expectations that are probably beyond realistic levels. Every defeat feels like the end of the world, but you want a passionate fanbase, it's apathy that's the killer. It's a by-product of failure when that passion turns into something negative, but when you can tap into it for a last-minute equaliser it's something hugely positive. In the click of a finger the mood will change, Elland Road will be utterly delirious, and we're all back again the following week to do it all again.'

15.	C. Palace	6
16.	Southampton	4
17.	Newcastle	3
18.	LEEDS	3
19.	Burnley	2
20.	Norwich	0

Leeds United 1 Watford 0

For the second game running I did a double-edged good deed, sacrificing my place in the Kop so Lucca's friend could stand with him, while I took his ticket in the East Upper. My generosity allowed the lads to watch the game together, but it suited me too because I was ill and better off sat in serenity rather than standing all game, inevitably screaming and shouting. I also sacrificed my free lift so as not to infect my dad, though even this thoughtful act was double-edged. With my marathon only two weeks away saturated fats were forbidden, and I knew I wouldn't be able to resist fish and chips if I caught a whiff of Park Fisheries.

I was intrigued to see Bielsaball from up in 'the gods', and the bird's eye view of El Loco's unique tactics was quite the spectacle. When in possession his players formed a big circle around the pitch, with midfielders Dallas and Klich practically up front with Rodrigo, the full-backs and wingers down the sides and the centre-backs at the bottom, leaving Kalvin Phillips looking like the piggy in the middle but performing the opposite role. It was wonderful to behold, especially as the tactics worked so well. Leeds were at concert pitch and produced a performance that made a mockery of the embryonic Premier League table that portrayed them as relegation fodder. From the first minute to the last they battered Watford, who just couldn't cope with the relentless pressing from Bielsa's vibrant front five.

There would have been an avalanche of goals but for chronic wastefulness in the final third, though one goal always looked like it might be enough and it came when Diego Llorente converted from a scrappy first-half corner. A large slice of fortune was required to ensure it was enough, with a Watford equaliser ruled out for the slightest infringement on Liam Cooper as Meslier fumbled a corner off his captain's head and into the goal. Tyler Roberts came within inches of putting the game to bed with a spectacular scissor kick that crashed off the bar, but United claimed their first win of the season regardless; their first in 19 weeks.

It had been 19 months since a packed Elland Road crowd were last sent home with the warm glow of that winning feeling, and sharing the experience with 35,000 other Leeds fans transformed the experience beyond recognition compared to watching a victory on TV, when with a click of the wife's fingers you're back in the room and reality bites again. The triumphant cheer that greets the final whistle, the pride as players and fans engage in a lap of mutual appreciation, the happy chirps of the fleeing flock on Lowfields Road; you can bask in the glory of it all night and look forward to watching the highlights later, safe in the knowledge that the memories will carry you through the working week.

It had been 18 years, almost to the day, since Leeds fans went to Elland Road on a Saturday and watched a Premier League victory. On 4 October 2003, Seth Johnson was the hero (words I never thought I'd write), scoring both goals in a 2-1 win over Blackburn Rovers, who had Dwight Yorke and Andy Cole trying to party like it was 1999. It blew my mind when I discovered this stat, especially when imagining the next Leeds United home win on *Match of the Day* would come in October 2039. The thought was inconceivable, and portrayed just how long-suffering the Leeds fans had been, before being blessed by the presence of El Loco.

Southampton 1 Leeds United 0

The secret was out. On his international debut Raphinha entered the fray with Brazil trailing 1-0 in Venezuela, and by the end he had claimed two assists, with a third ruled out by VAR, and he'd set up the action that led to a penalty in a 3-1 victory. A few days later Raphinha made his full debut, scoring twice in a 4-1 victory against Uruguay at the iconic Maracanã Stadium in Rio de Janeiro. A star was born.

After the match, Brazil's manager, Tite, publicly thanked Marcelo Bielsa for his work with the winger, while the Brazilian press hailed their new messiah, whose link-up play with Neymar drew sensationalised comparisons with the Ronaldo–Rivaldo partnership from the turn of the century. 'Raphinha is everything we have desperately needed from a right-winger for years. He has the flair and end product. He is the true essence of *joga bonito* [the beautiful game].' High praise indeed from one Brazilian news outlet.

It was the early hours of Friday morning (GMT) when Raphinha lit up the Maracanã, yet he made it to Southampton in time for the traditional Saturday 3pm kick-off. In time, but not in condition to play, and neither was Kalvin Phillips who hadn't recovered from the hip injury that deprived him of more England caps. Injury had also deprived Patrick Bamford of another chance with England, or perhaps it saved him the ignominy of being dropped after one goalless appearance vs Andorra. Junior Firpo was another addition to the injury list, and with Luke Ayling still recovering and Robin Koch in America for an operation on his, as The Great Man put it, 'rebellious pubis', United were once again down to the bare bones.

Yet no amount of injuries could excuse a performance on the south coast that was gallingly bad, arguably the most abject of El Loco's reign as Southampton claimed their first victory of the season with a simple 1-0 win. We had seen similar performances in the previous season (no coincidence that they came when Phillips was missing) but in 150 games we had never seen a Bielsa side register as few shots as the three they mustered at St Mary's, except for Manchester City away with ten men, when Leeds scored from their only two attempts. According to the doom-mongers on Twitter, 17th-placed Leeds were in dire straits, but I didn't believe a word of it, preferring to presume we just needed our best players back.

Thankfully I had another event to distract me from the social media misery pit. The following day was the Yorkshire Marathon, where I atoned for my failure to run a marathon prior to returning to Elland Road by raising nearly £1,500 for Target Ovarian Cancer, in honour of a family friend, Simone, who had tragically died just a few weeks earlier. The support I received really spurred me on (it sounds cheesy, but it really is true!) and I managed to achieve the standard target for a beginner, a sub-four-hour time. It was a true Hollywood ending as I sprinted down the home straight, crossing the line with arms outstretched at the very moment the race clock struck the four-hour mark. It was a wonderful way to finish, though not quite as dramatic as it sounds because, starting at the back, it had taken me seven minutes to cross the start line and I was fully aware that my official finishing time was a very satisfying three hours and 53 minutes.

Leeds United 1 Wolverhampton Wanderers 1

The week after the marathon was spent gorging on everything I'd deprived myself of for the past two months, but what I craved most was fish and chips, and a glorious return to Park Fisheries deserved to be washed down with a celebratory beer (I had 53 alcohol-free days to make up for). So I headed down to the Centenary Pavilion for the first time since lockdown and was pleased to be able to walk straight in without having to buy a beer token, as you did in the Old Normal. On entry the whole place seemed a lot more formal, but I put this down to a Premier League upgrade and headed straight for the bar, where I was impressed to see Birra Moretti on tap (previously it was Carling, Tetley's or Strongbow). I was even more impressed when the barmaid started pouring my pint into an actual glass rather than a plastic cup, and it finally dawned on me that something was seriously amiss when I got my card out to pay. 'Oh no,' said the lovely lady who served me, 'you only have to pay for spirits, sir.' I took my free pint and found a little table to stand at while I properly assessed my surroundings, which was when the lightbulb finally flashed – I'd wandered into corporate hospitality! Perhaps I could have stayed and drank them dry, but I decided to quit while I was ahead and quickly downed my pint before heading for the comforts of the Old Normal, paying out of my own pocket for a horrible pint of Tetley's in the Kop bar.

Wolves had been a real nuisance last season, their two spawny deflected goals earning 1-0 victories that effectively cost Leeds European qualification, and they were even more annoying in the flesh. Having turned Leeds around at kick-off, they proceeded to open the scoring against the run of play thanks to another spawny deflection, then, with only ten minutes on the clock, so began the time-wasting, the diving, and Conor Coady's fake head injuries. He had done it in the previous meeting between the sides, and when he hit the deck motionless in the penalty area after a shot hit his head, only to get up unharmed once the game had been stopped (and the pressure relieved), it sent me into a frenzy. I was hopping around the aisle of N11 like Basil Fawlty, only with no branch in my hand and no car to take my anger out on.

Early in the second half an appallingly late and cynical foul on Raphinha was only punished with a free kick, although the replay clearly showed the defender deliberately digging his studs into the Brazilian's ankle. If the Leeds players had surrounded the ref, or if Bielsa and his staff had bounced around their technical area waving their arms (or invaded the pitch like Jürgen Klopp), it would have led to a VAR review and a straight red card, but their respect for the officials was punished as VAR were asleep at the wheel. The defender walked away scot-free while Raphinha hobbled down the tunnel, his afternoon over.

Raphinha had been the shining light in an otherwise ordinary performance by Leeds, and without their Brazilian talisman Elland Road feared the worst. However, in adversity the ground often comes to the fore, and the crowd was suddenly ignited. 'Champions of Europe' swept around the stadium like wildfire, and the passion of the terraces transcended on to the pitch as the Whites were sparked into life. Rodrigo suddenly clicked into 'Pablo Mode', Stuart Dallas regained his confidence and became a menace down the left, while youngster Crysencio Summerville showed his potential with a menacing performance down the right. Then there was Joe Gelhardt, aka 'Joffy'.

In his first 30 minutes on the Elland Road pitch, Joffy had a greater impact than any other young home debutant I had seen in over 30 years of watching the club. With Leeds attacking the South Stand it was difficult to get a clear impression, but every time the number 30 got the ball things happened. His thunderous drive was miraculously saved, another attempt flashed over the bar, and on another occasion he seemed to meander around the penalty box with the ball glued to his feet for minutes rather than seconds, but couldn't quite get his shot away. Then, deep into injury time, 19-year-old Gelhardt picked the ball up 40 yards from goal. A 17-year-old Wayne Rooney once picked the ball up on the same blade of grass, brilliantly turned Eirik Bakke, drove into the box and fired past Nigel Martyn, and Joffy was on his way to replicating the goal until he was bundled to the floor in the penalty box. The referee pointed to the spot, and with our hearts in our mouths, desperate for Joffy's magnificent play to get its just desserts, Rodrigo calmly sent the keeper the wrong way before losing his head in the celebrations, booting the corner flag and snapping it in two. It was only a point on the board and Leeds remained just one place above the drop zone, but it had been a pulsating ending and Elland Road had a new hero; a stocky little rosy-cheeked teenager from Liverpool.

In his post-match presser, Marcelo Bielsa spoke of the 'ferocious desire' of his team and credited 'the public' for their decisive contribution to help change the game. The Great Man could take a lot of credit himself. His preference for a small 18-man squad was coming under increasing scrutiny, but if Bielsa ran a 25-man squad like his peers, Joe Gelhardt would almost certainly have chosen a different destination when Wigan's administrators offered him up for less than a million quid. It was more evidence that El Loco always knows best, he just sometimes works in mysterious ways.

Norwich City 1 Leeds United 2

A limp and lacklustre midweek defeat to Arsenal put paid to United's hopes of a deep run in the League Cup, and Saturday's results dragged them back into the bottom three ahead of the Sunday lunchtime trip to Carrow Road. Sections of the media billed this match as 'must win' for Leeds, but that said more about the inadequacy of the opponents than the impact the result would have on the final league table. Norwich had won the Championship at a canter in the previous season, but either side of that success they were winless in their last 19 Premier League games, with an aggregate score of 47-3.

Daniel Farke had presided over all 19 matches and his team's performance against Leeds was in line with their form; they were garbage. But they still had the better of a first half in which Leeds showed none of the ferocious desire that won them a point against Wolves. The visitors were second to every loose ball, losing all their 50-50s and struggling to string five passes together. Even the returning Kalvin Phillips was struggling, and at half-time I began to wonder whether we really were in for a long and difficult relegation battle.

In the second half my relegation fears were alleviated by a piece of magic from Raphinha. Brazil's new poster boy received the ball out wide and charged into the box, dinking through three challenges before threading his shot through the legs of two defenders and the goalkeeper, into the net. Happiness lasted less than a minute. Straight from kick-off some calamitous play from Shackleton and Meslier gifted Norwich a cheap corner, some calamitous marking gifted them a cheap equaliser, and my relegation fears were elevated to new heights. Good teams simply don't behave like this!

Bad teams do though, and two minutes later Rodrigo was celebrating with the passion and intensity he often lacked in open play after Tim Krul reciprocated Leeds's generosity by allowing the Spaniard's dipping 30-yard drive to slip through his butterfingers and into the net. It felt like a case of 'who wants to go down more?' but once back in the lead Leeds regained their composure and deservedly returned to Yorkshire with three vital points.

'It wasn't pretty, but who gives a shit?' No, these were not the words of Marcelo Bielsa. It was the tweet of captain Liam Cooper, and although I appreciated the sentiment I couldn't agree. The result was pleasing but the performance had been frightening. Every player seemed to be out of form and the Bielsaball we had become accustomed to was nowhere to be seen. There could be no denying it had been a hugely disappointing start to the season, but I remained convinced that last season's Leeds United were in there somewhere, just waiting to burst out.

November 2021

Bryn Law – 'It has been suggested that one of the differences the players noticed when the fans returned was the difficulty in communicating on the pitch. The players had been able to pass on information to each other very easily the previous season but now they couldn't hear each other, and communication was very important for the way Leeds played.'

15.	Aston Villa	10
16.	Watford	10
17.	LEEDS	10
18.	Burnley	7
19.	Newcastle	4
20.	Norwich	2

Leeds United 1 Leicester City 1

Leicester had made an indifferent start to the season, but this was still going to be a very difficult game for an out-of-sorts Leeds team, especially with no let-up in the injury list. Shackleton and Gelhardt had joined Ayling, Firpo, Koch and Bamford on the sidelines, but better news was the inclusion of Adam Forshaw, for his first start in over two years. Marcelo Bielsa rated Forshaw as the best player in the Leeds squad when he arrived at Elland

Road, and not only did he believe he could excel in the Premier League like his Championship team-mates had, he even felt Forshaw's style of play would suit a Champions League team.

Making it into a Bielsa line-up is no mean feat, and Forshaw being named in the starting 11 must have meant he was 100 per cent fit and 100 per cent sharp. But could he really still do it at such a high level, at 30 years old, after such a long absence? The answer was emphatic. Without a hint of sentiment Forshaw was named man of the match, and his presence alongside Kalvin Phillips in midfield gave United a solid base on which to dominate, resulting in the best performance of the season. High-octane pressing kept Leicester firmly on the back foot; they struggled to play out from the back, couldn't play through midfield, and any hopeful balls for Jamie Vardy to chase were expertly dealt with by Cooper and Llorente. Midway through the half Raphinha's in-swinging free kick evaded everyone and nestled in the corner, giving Leeds an advantage that should have been the springboard to a resounding victory, but just seven seconds after the restart Harvey Barnes curled in an exquisite equaliser.

Barnes's goal punctured the atmosphere and the performance, but after half-time Leeds raised their game again, and for 15 minutes they perhaps reached new heights. Their non-stop tenacity suffocated Leicester, leading to wave after wave of attacks. This was Bielsaball at full throttle and Elland Road was rocking. A goal would have blown the roof off, but Harrison kneed over an open goal from two yards, Rodrigo volleyed wide from six yards, and Dan James's finishing belonged in Headingley.

After surviving the 15-minute onslaught Leicester grew in confidence, and in the closing stages it was the visitors in the ascendancy. Fears of a sucker punch grew, but when the blow was landed the incompetence of VAR came to Leeds's rescue. Iheanacho's header was ruled out for a fractional offside, but Stockley Park had drawn their lines on a freeze frame that was a split second after Vardy's near-post flick-on, and when contact was actually made it seemed logical that Iheanacho would have been onside. Coming on the anniversary of Bamford's 'offside' goal at Crystal Palace, the reprieve was as poetic as it was fortunate.

The point gained nudged Leeds up to 15th, but they had missed a great opportunity to lift themselves away from danger. Nevertheless, in contrast to Cooper's tweet after the previous game, I didn't 'give a shit' that Leeds had only drawn. They had delivered a vintage performance, and with Scouse Lazarus Forshaw in midfield I was sure Bielsa's boys were ready to climb the table and challenge at the top again.

Tottenham Hotspur 2 Leeds United 1

The 'new manager bounce' was alive and kicking in the Premier League, with Steven Gerrard (Aston Villa), Dean Smith (Norwich) and Claudio Ranieri (Watford) completing a hat-trick of home wins on Saturday afternoon. It might have been 'a Viduka', but Eddie Howe (Newcastle) was forced to watch his home debut on TV due to a positive Covid test, and without him his new team were held to a 2-2 draw.

Antonio Conte (Tottenham) was looking to add his name to the list on Sunday evening, and his hopes were boosted by the surprise absence of Raphinha. A more pleasant surprise for the Leeds fans was Joe Gelhardt getting the nod to start up front in the continued absence of Patrick Bamford. Joffy became the fourth player charged with filling Bamford's boots in the last four games, a surefire sign of United's struggles when their only out-and-out striker wasn't there to lead the line. When the game commenced there was an even bigger surprise as Kalvin Phillips was deployed in the heart of defence, tasked with keeping Harry Kane quiet. The wantaway £150m-rated striker can't have come up against many better defenders than Phillips in his career, such was the expertise of the Yorkshire Pirlo's performance. Kane barely got a kick in the first half, and his team-mates chased shadows as the lowly visitors played them off the park, their mojo looking fully restored. It took until the 44th minute but Leeds grabbed a deserved half-time lead when Jack Harrison's wicked low cross into the corridor of uncertainty was tapped home by Dan James, his first goal for the proper United. The Yorkshire-born Welshman had been a disappointment since his big-money move from our arch-rivals, but the goal reinvigorated him and suddenly James looked every bit a £25m player.

James remained Leeds's main threat in the second half but Spurs suddenly had lots of threatening players. They looked a different team to the passive, lethargic one from the first half and Leeds couldn't cope. The two goals that turned the game on its head were fortunate, but there could have been others, and despite registering 18 attempts on goal Leeds rarely threatened an equaliser. Bielsa tinkered to try and reassert some authority, but where the first half had been a tactical masterclass the second half was a mess, and El Loco's changes only made things worse.

The final result, a 2-1 defeat, meant United had dropped ten points from a winning position in 12 games this season, having dropped only six in the same circumstances through the entirety of the previous campaign. More significantly, it left the Whites on the brink of the relegation zone, yet I didn't feel too downbeat. I hadn't expected a positive result, nor had I expected Leeds to play so well with so many key players missing. My confidence in the lads remained high heading into a pivotal week.

Brighton & Hove Albion 0 Leeds United 0

A week containing games against Brighton, Crystal Palace and Brentford took on extra importance due to the run of fixtures that would follow. El Loco's men would face arguably the three most difficult fixtures in world football in the space of three weeks – Chelsea away, Manchester City away, and Liverpool away – with Arsenal at home crammed between them for good measure. This quirk in the fixture list piled the pressure on Leeds. Rather than targeting a positive week to kick-start their season, they simply had to pick up a decent points haul over the next seven days or risk sinking to the bottom of the Premier League by the turn of the year.

If the players weren't feeling the pressure the fans certainly were, with the vast majority demanding new signings in the upcoming January window. El Loco was always acutely aware of the murmurs from the fanbase and used the pre-Brighton press conference to defend his philosophy, with pre-prepared notes to ensure his explanation was succinct. While most managers would simply have pointed to the important players who were unavailable as the reasons for the struggles – an England international striker, a Spanish international forward, a German international defender, an influential right-back, and the new star of Brazilian football – Bielsa preferred to speak positively about the crop of youngsters who had stepped into the team – Joe Gelhardt, Crysencio Summerville, Charlie Cresswell and Cody Drameh – who had received opportunities to gain experience and prove their worth, therefore adding further strength to the squad.

It was a passionate and reasoned answer to a question that was never asked. Bielsa had previously explained that he only had 'the public' to answer to, and his explanations were not an attempt to appease the board or repress pressure from the media, he just wanted the supporters to understand his methods. He was also keen to highlight the fact his methods might not be the correct approach, delivering a line that was classic El Loco, 'I am not the owner of the truth.'

Due to an unsightly kit clash (the lilac of Leeds blending in with the blue and white of Brighton) this Saturday teatime game would have been a difficult watch no matter what, but a dismal performance by Leeds was even more nauseating. It took Brighton less than two minutes to carve out the first opening and the pattern for the rest of the first half barely wavered, with the home team's wayward finishing repeatedly letting United off the hook. The only Leeds player doing himself justice was Adam Forshaw, who not only outperformed his team-mates but outran everybody on the pitch. Having sat on the sidelines for two years, he was a true medical marvel.

At half-time I was relieved to be level, and relieved to see Junior Firpo relieved of his duties as the team trotted out for the second half. The left-back had failed to impress since arriving from Barcelona, but tonight he looked completely out of his depth as young Tariq Lamptey skinned him time and time again. Bielsa also withdrew Kalvin Phillips, and the double substitution brought a slight improvement after the break. Brighton were still the better side though, and a slight improvement in their finishing brought three brilliant saves from Meslier, who also required some assistance from the woodwork to keep his clean sheet intact.

Tyler Roberts came close to completing a 'smash and grab' for the visitors, but after a poor performance Bielsa was pulling no punches: 'A team performs consistently when they manage to mix creativity and organisation in proportion. It is my function to achieve this, and when it doesn't happen it is because I'm not doing it well.' The Great Man was perhaps being too hard on himself; after all, his team had earned a decent point away from home, which would become an excellent point if Leeds could follow it up with two home wins.

Leeds United 1 Crystal Palace 0

A winnable trilogy had turned into a must-win double, and first up were a Crystal Palace side who had made a good start to the season under new boss Patrick Vieira, with Leeds's prime summer target, Conor Gallagher, excelling in midfield to such an extent that he had broken into the England squad. The Whites' failure to capture Gallagher on loan came in for less criticism than their decision to forego any alternatives, and Andrea Radrizzani copped the brunt of the fans' frustrations when tweeting that Adam Forshaw was the answer. Forshaw's triumphant return had consequently earned our owner a multitude of apologies, and a bucketload more were bound to follow if Forshaw could upstage Gallagher tonight.

It was a cold winter night at Elland Road, an 8.15pm kick-off thanks to Amazon Prime, and when the match finally got under way United's determination to make up for their disappointing showing at Brighton was clear to see. The home team were full of energy, but it took until early in the second half to carve the visitors open, when Dan James laid a chance on a plate. Maddeningly, Rodrigo was caught between sliding the ball into the net and skipping around the keeper, and simply prodded the ball harmlessly wide. At the other end an even clearer chance fell to Christian Benteke, but the beleaguered Belgian headed wide of an open goal from six yards.

With the clock ticking down I was prepared to accept what would, on paper, be a disappointing point. I was proud of Leeds's performance, and took heart from the improving form of James, Forshaw's bossing of Gallagher in midfield, and the fantastic attitude of the rest of the team. Scoring goals remained the problem – Tyler Roberts had become the fifth player to lead the line in six games since Bamford's injury (all failing to score) – but they kept fighting right to the end of injury time, when a flurry of corners ended with Diego Llorente frantically pleading with the referee to award a penalty for handball. I hadn't noticed an infringement but the exuberance of the protests led me to think there was a chance it might be given, although my sworn hatred of VAR prevented me from getting excited at the prospect of profiting from the technology, and there was certainly no way I would join in with the Kop's shameless chants of 'VAR! VAR! VAR!' I couldn't even bring myself to cheer when the referee was instructed to rewatch the incident on his monitor, but the whole of Elland Road erupted when he turned back to the pitch and pointed to the spot.

It's pretty daft how nervous you get for a last-minute penalty, with the fear of missing totally overshadowing the excitement a glorious chance to win the game should bring. I was sick with nerves, but throughout the whole palaver Raphinha had stood calmly with ball in hand, patiently waiting to either take another corner or a penalty. When he stepped up to take the spot kick the ground fell silent, and I was certain he'd miss when he stuttered his run-up in a way that always fills supporters with dread. Yet it was the stutter that beat the keeper, leaving him flat-footed and helpless as Raphinha's strike bulged the net. The Kop went crazy, but rather than join in with the 'limbs' I stood motionless with clenched fists, feeling closer to bursting into tears than a fit of delirious delight. My fragile emotional state had been compounded by criticism of Bielsa in the aftermath of the Brighton game, with some fans not only questioning The Great Man's decisions but even his suitability for the job. I was so relieved, for the fans, for the players, and for myself, but most of all, for El Loco.

The final whistle was greeted by scenes of jubilation, with the players celebrating as exuberantly as the fans. 'FOLLOW, FOLLOW, FOLLOW. WE'VE GOT THE BEST CHUFFING TEAM IN THE WORLD! BAMFORD AND FIRPO, RAPHA RODRIGO, PHILLIPS THE YORKSHIRE PIRLO!' Elland Road's newest chant was sung on repeat throughout the players' lap of honour, and continued on the way out of the ground and all the way down Lowfields Road.

'Always a victory brings happiness,' said a visibly relieved Bielsa after the match, 'and in a human group happiness is indispensable. We can breathe again.' Maybe so, Marcelo, but not for long.

December 2021

Bryn Law – 'Leeds had gone through the two previous seasons without any major problems, but when injuries hit key players the lack of depth in the squad was exposed. Kalvin Phillips was the fulcrum and you'd also lost your leading goalscorer, with no like-for-like replacement for either of these players.'

15.	LEEDS	15
16.	Southampton	15
17.	Watford	13
18.	Burnley	10
19.	Norwich	10
20.	Newcastle	7

Leeds United 2 Brentford 2

A very difficult season had tested the faith of the Elland Road faithful, yet on the first Sunday of December Leeds had the tranquil waters of mid-table in their sights. Victory over Brentford would hoist United to the top of the bottom half, if only temporarily, and bring them to the same points total they'd gathered at the same stage of the previous season, which would beg the question, 'What was all the fuss about?'

The fuss over injuries was certainly dissipating. With Patrick Bamford returning to the bench and Luke Ayling returning to the starting 11 the only absentees were Pascal Struijk and Robin Koch, but even they would both be back in full training within days. It was the closest that Marcelo Bielsa had been to having a fully fit squad in his entire tenure, but just 15 minutes into the first half captain Liam Cooper hobbled off holding his hamstring, and 15 minutes into the second half Kalvin Phillips did the same. We were back to square one.

The Championship battles with Brentford had all been tight affairs, and today was no different despite Thomas Frank arriving at Elland Road without his two star men – top scorer Ivan Toney and goalkeeper David Raya – and on a terrible run of one win in nine. At half-time Leeds were a Tyler Roberts goal to the good, but as Phillips pulled up with injury a lovely goal by Sergi Canós put them 2-1 behind. The Kop were infuriated by Canós's deliberately antagonising celebrations, and a plastic cup hurled from the terraces brought some light relief when it landed square on his peroxided head, but of far greater importance was the fact Leeds were staring down the barrel of a disastrous result.

The final half an hour was spent in Brentford territory, but their defence, led by former Elland Road cult hero Pontus Jansson, was rarely troubled. Patrick Bamford was introduced but barely touched the ball until a 94th-minute Raphinha corner was flicked on by Ayling and flicked in off the crossbar by the striker's knee. A second injury-time goal in four days had Elland Road in raptures, but nobody was going crazier than Bamford, who galloped down the touchline, waving his shirt around his head before flinging it into the air and getting mobbed by his team-mates.

Once the euphoria died down it was time to reflect on another disappointing afternoon. The result wasn't terrible and neither was the performance, but it was a far cry from the swashbuckling football that had lit up the Premier League from behind closed doors. If it had felt like watching our Championship selves, it was probably because we practically were. Phillips, Forshaw and Klich had been Leeds's midfield in all three of Bielsa's home games against Brentford, and Cooper, Ayling, Dallas, Harrison, Roberts and Bamford had all played too, as had Pontus, for one team or the other. United had spent 18 months in the Premier League and £150m on transfers, but I now wondered whether the squad was any better for it. Ben White, Gjanni Alioski and a younger Pablo Hernández would have walked into today's team, and Kemar Roofe and Jansson would surely have been handy to have too.

Regardless of the negativity, a six-point cushion ahead of the relegation places was reassuring, and I assumed it would be enough to keep our heads above water even if Leeds took zero points from the crazy run-up to Christmas. Nothing was going particularly right this season, but Bielsa's boys were just about managing to do enough.

Chelsea 3 Leeds United 2

Just when it seemed that Leeds were through the other side of an injury-ravaged period, Marcelo Bielsa delivered news that was so bad it was almost comical. Liam Cooper and Kalvin Phillips's hamstring injuries would keep them sidelined for three months, and during the wild celebration of his comeback goal Patrick Bamford had also suffered hamstring damage, ruling him out for several weeks. You couldn't make it up! And that wasn't the end of it. Rodrigo was also injured, Robin Koch was ill, and Pascal Struijk remained unavailable too. From having an almost clean bill of health four days earlier, suddenly Leeds were more hit than they'd been all season, and just in time for the most challenging run of fixtures imaginable.

While the Twitterati panicked, Bielsa delivered a stirring war cry in his pre-match presser, 'My position is one of optimism and strength. It is a conclusion I draw when perceiving the mood of this team. I understand that, in adversity, one of the possible responses is fatalism, but there is another option: optimism, hope and fight.' Go on, Marcelo!

The Great Man's words certainly seemed to strike a chord with his remaining players, who responded with a performance that was as typical as it was unlikely. Their hustling and hounding of Chelsea was a joy to see, and they took the lead through a Raphinha penalty, with the Brazilian's stutter again leaving the goalkeeper flat-footed in a carbon copy of his spot kick ten days earlier. With seven goals in 14 games this season, there was no doubt who was carrying the torch for this ailing team.

It took Leeds until the 42nd minute to make their first mistake, and seconds later Mason Mount was 'shushing' the away fans having equalised in front of them. It was a dispiriting way to end a wonderful first half, and an infuriating start to the second when VAR controversially awarded Chelsea a penalty following Raphinha's scruffy tackle in the box. It wasn't 'clear and obvious' and seemed to fall well below the threshold for overturning decisions.

A pulsating battle continued, and with just a goal in the game and time running out, Bielsa turned to Joe Gelhardt. It was his last throw of the dice and he rolled double sixes. Within 90 seconds Leeds's slick interplay broke through Chelsea's defence, and Gelhardt nipped in ahead of Thiago Silva – a legendary centre-back twice the youngster's age – to turn Tyler Roberts's excellent low cross into the net. It was vintage Bielsaball, what a way to score your first Premier League goal, and what character Leeds had shown; fortitude and optimism rewarded.

With only five minutes remaining Chelsea were on the verge of dropping two vital points in their three-way title race with Liverpool and Manchester City, so Thomas Tuchel turned to a substitutes' bench containing £300m of talent (Leeds's nine substitutes cost a total of £2.5m) and on came his £100m summer signing, Romelu Lukaku. Bielsa responded by immediately sending on teenager Charlie Cresswell to nullify Belgium's all-time top scorer, but just as Leeds were about to claim a fantastic point, a needless flick of Klich's boot sent Antonio Rüdiger tumbling in the box and Chelsea were awarded the softest of soft injury-time penalties.

Jorginho converted again to steal the points, and at the final whistle the indignation of the Leeds players boiled over, resulting in a 22-man brawl that provided a fitting encore to an intoxicating spectacle.

Despite the injustice of the result, I loved this game. For so long our bitter rivalries had been with Cardiff, Millwall and Huddersfield, but this battle of Stamford Bridge transported me back to the 1990s, with Leeds fighting against the elite in a cauldron of noise and hate. I was so proud of my team, and so too was El Loco, 'The performance today allows us to think we can recover the version that allows us to compete with the best teams.' God bless you, Marcelo.

Manchester City 7 Leeds United 0

Three days after battling the Champions League winners, Leeds now faced the Champions League runners-up, and English champions. Lewis was back from Canada for Christmas, so I added Manchester City to the list of supporters' clubs I belonged to and booked four tickets in the home end for us, my dad, and Lewis's nephew, Joseph (his first live game). Lewis and I had been to Manchester City away twice, enjoying two handsome victories back in the David O'Leary years, but a 9-2 aggregate lead would be wiped out in 90 catastrophic minutes.

The Etihad Stadium looked spectacular from the outside, with its swirling pillars – clearly modelled on the iconic San Siro – lighting up the black night sky. It was half a world away from City's old Maine Road ground, and from Elland Road too, and in a moment of weakness it made me long for an upgrade of our tired old home. An upgrade of the Kop's beer choices certainly wouldn't go amiss, but our enjoyment of the locally brewed pilsners in the Colin Bell Stand was ruined by the team news, with City's line-up striking fear into us all. Jack Grealish had pulled up no trees since his £100m move from Aston Villa, but a front five that also included Kevin De Bruyne, Riyad Mahrez, Phil Foden and Bernardo Silva could tear any side to shreds, not least one that was as disjointed as Leeds, with the whole spine of their team in the treatment room.

We headed for our seats on the very top row of the upper tier and were subjected to a pre-match lights show which, amid my respect for an impressive stadium, made me so thankful for our decrepit bear pit in Beeston. The lights show was painful to watch, but the real pain started once it had finished. Silva had already missed an open goal by the time Foden opened the scoring after seven minutes, and after 13 minutes Grealish was afforded a free header from six yards out and doubled the lead. The match was already over as a spectacle; it was simply a case of how many City would score, and the answer was 'shitloads'.

By half-time De Bruyne had made it 3-0, and within minutes of the restart Mahrez's deflected shot made it 4-0. Being on the back row was a saving grace of sorts as we didn't have to stand up politely every time City scored; mind you, the home fans in the Bell End barely erected themselves once the fourth went in. On the hour De Bruyne hammered in a stunning long-range strike for 5-0, John Stones scored the sixth, and his centre-back partner Nathan Aké was left free from a corner to make it 7-0 with 15 minutes still remaining. The Leeds defence was dazed and demoralised, and I feared conceding double figures, but they managed to hold themselves together and register only the joint worst defeat in the club's history (but the worst in my lifetime).

At the full-time whistle Bielsa stood motionless at the edge of his technical area, watching on as the players thanked the travelling fans for their unrelenting support in the face of the ultimate humiliation. There he remained until the last of his players left the pitch, and only then did he follow them into the dressing room. Some saw this as a silent rollicking from the manager, but to me this was

El Loco refusing exoneration; he did not deserve to suffer any less than his players.

If anyone deserved to suffer less than the players it was the supporters, but roadworks on the M62 ensured we didn't get home until 1am. Three hours later, Alessandro was wide awake, and the suffering began again. What a night.

Leeds United 1 Arsenal 4

Well, it's been almost half a season since I last mentioned the C word, and I'd have snapped your hand off for that! The pandemic was never out of the news but life in the UK had been continuing as normal, until a highly contagious new Covid variant, Omicron (an anagram of moronic, just to fuel the 'scamdemic' conspiracies), swept through the nation and decimated the pre-Christmas football schedule. It was still unknown how dangerous Omicron was, but with infection rates soaring to an all-time high it seemed inevitable that restrictions would be re-introduced.

With many clubs struck by Covid outbreaks there was talk of a 'circuit break' in the Premier League season, but despite Leeds's injury crisis I was desperate for the show to go on, and desperate for the Whites to have the chance to atone for the Manchester City debacle. It was a Saturday evening kick-off and I spent all day waiting for the match to be called off, but by the time I set off for Elland Road Leeds v Arsenal was the only Premier League fixture to survive postponement.

Ironically, Leeds had more absentees than any of the Covid-ravaged clubs. Jamie Shackleton and Dan James hadn't recovered from their injuries sustained at Manchester City, while Junior Firpo was suspended having received his fifth yellow card of the season at the Etihad, taking the list of absentees up to nine. Then, in the last minute of the final training session on Friday, Charlie Cresswell dislocated his shoulder, and on the morning of the match Cresswell's intended centre-back partner, Diego Llorente, tested positive for Covid, and Luke Ayling reported feeling ill too! Had they kicked up a stink the match could have been called off, but Leeds soldiered on regardless, with Bielsa thrusting Robin Koch into action after a four-month absence, with only a week's training under his belt, alongside the ailing Ayling in defence.

The absentees weren't limited to the pitch either. My dad was worried about Omicron so gave up his ticket, enabling my mate Gaz to take his Leeds-mad son, Arthur, to his first live game. Lucca had to work so his ticket went to Lewis's girlfriend, Amanda, who was due to land from Canada on the morning of the game and was desperate to experience Elland Road. However, due to heavy fog at Leeds Bradford airport, and a shortage of bus drivers at neighbouring airports, her flight was cruelly diverted back to Amsterdam, ruling her out of the match. If Lewis wanted Amanda Hugandkiss when Leeds scored, he'd have to settle for me.

A light blanket of fog hung inside the stadium, providing a dramatic backdrop for an electric atmosphere. Leeds started well, forcing a corner within a minute, but it was all downhill from there. Five minutes later the injury list grew as Jack Harrison hobbled off the pitch, replaced by Crysencio Summerville – the most experienced of the nine substitutes and the only one to have played in the Premier League (for 69 minutes in total). The least experienced substitute was 15-year-old Archie Gray, a year 11 pupil at my old school, a former classmate of Lucca's, and the great nephew of the great Eddie Gray. With such a threadbare team it was no surprise that Leeds lost this match, but it was distressing to see them carved open time and time again by a classy Arsenal side. By half-time Leeds were 3-0 down, and it could have been 7-0 were it not for the heroics of Illan Meslier.

'The knowledgeable Elland Road crowd won't boo them off,' predicted Lewis, and he was right. It had been a calamitous performance, but according to Marcelo Bielsa the Leeds fans are at their most generous in adversity, and the manager's name duly rang around the stadium during the second half. They wanted El Loco to know he retained their full support despite two shameful results, and when Raphinha stepped up to take a penalty after Gelhardt was hacked down by Ben White, Bielsa's name rang around the stadium again. This time it was a message to the rest of the country, who would all see this moment on *Match of the Day* (especially as this was the only match of the day), that Elland Road has nothing but love for the Argentinian. Raphinha angrily blasted the spot kick into the top corner and for a short period there was a glimmer of hope, but Emile Smith Rowe, the man who sealed Leeds's promotion with a goal for Huddersfield Town, sealed the match by coming off the bench to make it 4-1. Job done, but not for the Leeds fans.

For the final minutes the whole ground swung scarves around their heads and chanted 'WE ALL LOVE LEEDS!' It was a great sight, and a great gesture to keep it going through the final whistle and throughout the players' lap of appreciation (not honour on this occasion), until the last of them had disappeared down the tunnel. It was a special moment, one that could define the era. This support was unique, something I'd never seen before, and a reflection of Bielsa's seismic impact on Leeds United.

'For the fans to not let go of the team's hand was an act of love.' Only Marcelo could have put it so beautifully, and coming days after The Great Man himself had refused to let go of the team's hand at Manchester City was so poignant. My team had just conceded 11 goals in four days, but I'd never been prouder to be a Leeds United fan.

January 2022

BRYN LAW – 'When you're doing club commentary you're duty bound to keep trying to be upbeat, so a 7-0 defeat is as hard as it gets. What do you do with this thing? You can't stop talking, that's not allowed, so you've just got to plough on. The contrast between Manchester City the previous season and this one could not have been greater.'

15.	Everton	19
16.	LEEDS	16
17.	Watford	13
18.	Burnley	11
19.	Newcastle	11
20.	Norwich	10

Leeds United 3 Burnley 1

It had taken three and a half years, ten first-team absentees, and fixtures against three of the most expensive squads ever assembled for Marcelo Bielsa to lose three league games in a row at Leeds United. When I tweeted this it went viral (if 2,000 likes counts as being viral) and I was ready to reel it out again the following week, only changing the threes to fours, as the depleted

Whites were heading to fortress Anfield. Or so they thought.

To be fair, I never really thought we would be going to Anfield. Football was back behind closed doors in Scotland and Wales, and I expected the same for England as Covid cases continued to soar. However, with hospitalisations still low, Boris Johnson confirmed there would be no further restrictions imposed for Christmas, and this milder mutation of the virus brought renewed hope that the pandemic was finally coming to an end, once and for all.

I was thrilled that football would continue. Even though Leeds were enduring such a difficult season I was still loving Bielsaball and looked forward to each and every match, even a near certain Boxing Day drubbing at Anfield. But shortly after the PM's announcement came the news Liverpool vs Leeds had been postponed, because Leeds had half a dozen Covid cases in the squad and on top of their injury crisis it was impossible to field a team. I was gutted, and to rub salt into the wounds the home game against Aston Villa on 28 December was off too. My Christmas was ruined, but for the Leeds squad a two-week Christmas break was undeniably a blessing, refreshing them ahead of a huge six-pointer against Burnley on New Year's Day.

Sean Dyche's perennial strugglers had only won once in their last 19 Premier League games, yet they were only five points behind Leeds with two games in hand. Be that as it may, Bielsa refused to get carried away with the importance of the result, simply describing the match as 'an opportunity to redirect where the campaign is going'. El Loco's outlook was unique at the best of times but amid

Leeds's struggles his eccentricity was amplified, and in his pre-match presser he bemoaned his own performance (apparently he wasn't giving the club value for money) and refused to complain about the injury crisis that had forced him to regularly pick a substitutes' bench with a total value of under £5m. In stark contrast, his peers were constantly complaining, with Jürgen Klopp and Thomas Tuchel the worst offenders – slating England's traditional Christmas period for damaging 'player welfare' and calling the fixture 'pile-up' (two games a week) 'impossible', this despite regularly having over £200m of talent sat on the bench.

On New Year's Day the value of Bielsa's bench was boosted to £30m by Dan James, who had worked hard but failed to impress during his stint as an emergency centre-forward. His Wales team-mate Tyler Roberts got the nod up front, meaning Joe Gelhardt was also left on the bench and effectively remained fourth-choice striker despite his prodigious talent. That was a situation that frustrated me, but The Great Man knew best, and it was comforting to know there were two genuine game-changers on the bench, a luxury Leeds hadn't had all season.

After a slow start the match changed when Raphinha pinged a 50-yard effort towards Wayne Hennessey's goal. From the moment it left his foot you knew the keeper was in trouble, and as it arched towards the top corner the Welshman was clearly beaten. Sadly, the ball just clipped the top of the bar, but the effort received a rousing reception from Elland Road and the team suddenly clicked into 'rampant mode'.

The Burnley goal was subsequently peppered, and when Jack Harrison fired into the Kop net Leeds had the half-time lead they thoroughly deserved, but ten minutes after the break Maxwell Cornet drilled home a 30-yard free kick to stun Elland Road into silence.

With the scores level Leeds's season was at a crossroads; the next goal was critical, and two minutes after the equaliser Tyler Roberts became the latest injury casualty. As he limped off the pitch all eyes were transfixed on the substitutes' bench in anticipation of who would replace him: would it be James or Joffy? The roar around the stadium when Gelhardt got the signal was spine-tingling, and sparked United back into life.

James didn't have to wait long before joining the action too, and his first touch presented Raphinha with a sitter. The Brazilian's left foot had almost scored from the halfway line, but his right foot couldn't find an empty net from the corner of the six-yard box. Raphinha soon atoned for his miss by winning a corner and taking it quickly to catch Burnley off guard. Klich squared to Stuart Dallas, and Dallas brilliantly buried a 20-yard first-time drive with his left foot, into the corner of the net, then buried himself into the ecstatic South Stand. What a way to mark your 250th appearance for the club.

With a slender lead it was time to anxiously clock-watch, and the announcement of five minutes of injury time was greeted by grumbles from the crowd. In the second of those minutes Mateusz Klich won possession in midfield, expertly turned his marker and popped the ball through the defender's legs to set Joe Gelhardt free. It was a wonderful piece of play by the Pole, and Gelhardt matched it by delivering a pinpoint cross, plumb on the head of his fellow substitute, Dan James. James used every muscle in his body to get as much power behind the header as he could, and when his Welsh team-mate in the Burnley goal palmed the ball into the air the world slipped into slow motion; 35,000 Yorkshiremen held their breath, and when the ball finally dropped into the corner of the net Elland Road went ballistic! The relief was euphoric, the points were safe, and the victory meant more to one man than anyone else.

Marcelo Bielsa's reaction to James's goal was a thing of sheer beauty. He first shook his fists, then embraced his coach, Pablo Quiroga, holding him tightly for what seemed an eternity, before finally letting go and resuming his 13-step pacing, up and down his technical area. We had seen such releases of emotion before, but this eclipsed them all. It was as intimate as any goal celebration could be, revealing the depth of Bielsa's love for Leeds United, and served as a reminder of how lucky we were that a manager of his calibre and standing in the game would never leave us, a struggling Premier League newcomer, not for anyone, nor any amount of money. God bless El Loco.

West Ham United 2 Leeds United 3

Having initially operated a case-by-case approach to fixture cancellations, the Premier League introduced a guideline that enabled clubs to cancel fixtures if they had fewer than 14 available players with Premier League experience, and in true 'modern football' spirit the clubs were taking advantage of this rule at every turn. Thus, nobody could be sure what their next fixture would be, although with two bites of the cherry Leeds could be pretty sure their next game would be West Ham away.

First up was an FA Cup third round tie, and thanks to a ticket allocation of 9,000 I managed to secure seats in the away end for me and George. We met outside my Airbnb in Camden and squeezed in three pints and a burger before heading to the ground, where we hoped to watch Leeds's first team against West Ham's reserves. To our surprise it was the exact opposite. Champions League-chasing West Ham – who were also still in the Europa League – fielded their full-strength side, while Bielsa rested his best players and gave debuts to 18-year-old centre-back Leo Hjelde, 19-year-old midfielder Lewis Bate, and 19-year-old forward Sam Greenwood. All three had joined the club since promotion to the Premier League, the most expensive of an influx of 'development squad' signings that were at the core of Leeds's long-term strategy: to pick up the best young talent and develop them into stars. Although I was interested to see what these boys could do, I was gutted Bielsa wasn't taking the FA Cup seriously, and further disheartened at the absence of the best youngster of all, Joe Gelhardt, who was injured and not even on the bench.

So it was little surprise the match was a damp squib, with the majority of it spent discussing the many idiosyncrasies of the London Stadium (mainly the ludicrously vast space between the Leeds fans in the top and bottom tiers). In the end a 2-0 defeat was as much as the Whites deserved, with the only memorable aspect being another shocking VAR decision when the offside Jarrod Bowen was deemed to be not interfering with play, despite clattering into Meslier when challenging for a loose ball that was slammed into the net seconds later.

The following Sunday Leeds returned to West Ham in the Premier League, and the fact I was following the game from the Women's Institute in Romanby, rather than the away end, aptly represented a polar opposite encounter. I was attending baby Rowan's christening, but my Smoggy mate Tom kept me up to date with events at the London Stadium, and it was a lovely surprise when he informed me of Jack Harrison's opening goal after only ten minutes.

Leeds had gone into this game with nine players unavailable – Cooper, Llorente, Cresswell, Shackleton, Phillips, Bamford, Roberts, Gelhardt and Greenwood (yes, all four strikers) – and I couldn't believe Tom, or his LiveScore app, when they told me both Junior Firpo and Adam Forshaw had limped off after just 20 minutes, replaced by Leo Hjelde and Lewis Bate. This had to be the worst injury curse since records began, and directly led to a hollow record for El Loco, who became the first manager to give Premier League debuts to eight teenagers in one season. There was no surprise the next time we checked the score – West Ham had equalised through last week's hero (villain), Jarrod Bowen, but another goal immediately popped up and I was stunned to see that Harrison had scored it. The patched-up visitors had restored their advantage!

At half-time we left the christening and drove home with the radio and our phones switched off, so I could watch the second half 'virtual live' when I got back. When West Ham equalised for a second time I considered watching an inevitable defeat on double speed, but Leeds's response was magnificent. Bate and Hjelde looked completely at ease against two of the league's form players, Bowen and Declan Rice, Pascal Struijk shackled the beastly goal machine Michail Antonio, while Leeds's three-pronged attack was a constant menace. Dan James made 47 sprints in the match, a new Premier League record, and although the man of the match award would go to Jack Harrison, Raphinha was the catalyst for a wonderful victory. With his trickery and inventiveness, the jewel in Leeds's crown was the thorn in West Ham's side, and he struck the post with a fantastic free kick before creating the winning goal with a beautifully weighted, Pablo-esque diagonal pass that Harrison dinked majestically over the keeper to complete a wonderful hat-trick.

The final action of a riveting game should have been an equaliser for Bowen, but instead of stooping to head into an empty net from three yards he tried to chest the ball over the line and sent it over the bar. Considering all their injuries (not to mention their six cursed years of misfortune in the capital) Leeds had earned their slice of luck, and successive league wins had built a soothing nine-point cushion ahead of the relegation zone.

The north London derby should have followed the Leeds match, but Arsenal managed to get it postponed despite only one of their players having Covid. Four were at the African Cup of Nations, one was suspended, and they loaned two players out in the days before the match, which took them over the Premier League's threshold for postponement. It was a blatant and brazen exploitation of the rules, and led to unanimous praise for the integrity and humility of Bielsa, who had continued without complaint despite naming a bench that included six teenagers, a 20-year-old, and a 15-year-old child. Under the circumstances this had to be considered one of the best results of The Great Man's tenure, just a few weeks since his lowest ebb.

Leeds United 0 Newcastle United 1

Since the trip to St James' Park in September everything and nothing had changed at Newcastle United. They were now the richest club in the world thanks to a controversial Saudi Arabian takeover, but old habits die hard, and the team were still deep in relegation trouble with only one win all season and reeling from an embarrassing FA Cup defeat at home to Cambridge United. It had been a relatively quiet January transfer window on Tyneside too. Amid lofty expectations of signing Kylian Mbappé and Erling Haaland, their only acquisitions had been 32-year-old right-back Kieran Trippier and 30-year-old target man Chris Wood, with just a week to go before deadline day. If Newcastle were going to save themselves they'd have to get busy quickly, both on and off the pitch.

At Elland Road there was no such wealth and no January signings whatsoever, yet everything felt rosy again. Bielsa's boys were back in the groove and a third successive Premier League win would move them on to 25 points, 11 clear of the bottom three and out of the relegation conversations, though I wouldn't be in the Kop to cheer the lads to victory. I'd received a generous offer to join my mates Adam and Isaac in corporate hospitality, and by 12.30pm we were enjoying a bottomless lunch in the Centenary Pavilion while former players were brought on to the stage in front of us to share their pre-match thoughts. Tony Dorigo, Jermaine Beckford, Dom Matteo, Mel Sterland, Steve Hodge, Neil Aspin and Matty Jones all predicted a comfortable victory for Leeds, setting off alarm bells in my head. Rarely is football so straightforward.

After an indulgent few hours I was happy for the extra comfort of the padded seats in the East Upper, and happy Leeds were forced to attack the Kop in the first half again, minimising the regret of not watching the game from my spiritual home. It was a half that was typical of so many we'd seen under Bielsa; wave after wave of Leeds attacks, but no cutting edge in the final third. Dan James was still on number nine duties and squandered the clearest opening, and the longer Patrick Bamford remained on the sidelines the clearer it became how much Leeds missed him. In fact, injury had enhanced Bamford's reputation even more than his 17 goals had in the previous season.

Despite filling our boots pre-match, one half-time pint wasn't deemed sufficient and we quickly poured two down our necks. It turned out to be a fatal decision for me. I was plagued by the dreaded double vision and had to cover one eye for the remainder of the game, though I might have been better off covering both. Leeds quickly ran out of ideas during a desperately disappointing second half, with their only chance again fluffed by makeshift striker James. Then, after 75 minutes of time wasting and little else ('The referee has the tools to stop it happening,' said El Loco after the game, in a subtle but exceedingly rare dig at the officials), Newcastle took the lead when a speculative Jonjo Shelvey free kick somehow evaded Meslier and nestled into the net to great despair. It was wholly undeserved, but there was no coming back and Eddie Howe's side grabbed a valuable three points that kept Leeds in the relegation mix.

By now the fears of a Covid-induced circuit break had subsided – Omicron was mild and the pandemic was slowly becoming a thing of the past – but due to their FA Cup exit, an international break, and the recently introduced midwinter break, the Leeds fans were forced to stew over this frustrating result for 17 days. Bielsa would be stewing too, but for the players it was a chance to rest, recuperate, and recover from injury, ahead of another daunting run of fixtures in February.

February 2022

Bryn Law – 'I began to get a real concern about where things were heading when Leeds started to concede quite a few goals quite easily. For whatever reason, the thing that had worked so spectacularly well in the season before had now completely stopped working, and you started to get the sense that the players were losing faith in the system. And the system was key, it was everything.'

15.	LEEDS	22
16.	Everton	19
17.	Norwich	16
18.	Newcastle	15
19.	Watford	14
20.	Burnley	12

Aston Villa 3 Leeds United 3

The transfer window passed with no incomings to strengthen Bielsa's squad, despite Cooper, Phillips and Bamford all being ruled out until March. It wasn't quite for the lack of trying, but the only target was American midfielder Brenden Aaronson and Red Bull Salzburg had no intention of selling, ahead of their upcoming first Champions League last-16 tie against the mighty Bayern

Munich. While acknowledging that new players would be welcome, Bielsa suggested it would cost more than £30m for any player who would improve the squad, and considering the heavy investments already made he didn't feel he could ask any more of the board and claimed to already have the resources to succeed in any case.

Judging by CEO Angus Kinnear's pre-Newcastle programme notes, the board and their manager were totally aligned, 'Many January options would not have been a material improvement on the emerging players and would block the development of our youngsters. Central to our long-term strategy is the ability to promise and deliver to young players a fast track to first-team football, as well as a culture where there is a belief in the process.' Kinnear concluded, 'It is better if our recruitment strategy is disagreed with by some fans, rather than misunderstood by many.' Unfortunately for Kinnear, most fans disagreed with the club's transfer strategy despite understanding it.

Aston Villa were the main club attracting admiring glances from the frustrated crop of Leeds fans. They had enjoyed a busy transfer window, topped off by manager Steven Gerrard successfully wooing his old pal, Philippe Coutinho, who joined on loan from Barcelona. Ahead of his first match-up with Marcelo Bielsa, Gerrard added his name to a long list of admirers by lavishing high praise on The Great Man, 'The Leeds players are living the dream to have the opportunity to play and compete in his style. They take it to every opponent, and they've got a world-class manager who's done a phenomenal job from where he took over to where he's got them to now.' As always, it was lovely to hear.

I settled in the lounge on a Wednesday evening and was delighted to see Leeds take an early lead thanks to a clinical Dan James finish from the edge of the box. The Whites were on top of their game and everything was going perfectly, until a long-range James effort crashed off the bar. Moments later, Coutinho found space in the box and produced a clinical finish of his own, then produced a piece of magic to play in Jacob Ramsey, who duly fired past Meslier. After another counter-attack and another clinical Ramsey finish, Leeds found themselves 3-1 down, 15 minutes after a lick of paint had denied them a 2-0 lead.

To say I was shell-shocked wouldn't quite be true. Falling foul of three-goal salvos was not an uncommon phenomenon for Bielsa's team, but having dominated the half it felt very cruel. Thankfully, the Football Gods were feeling sympathetic. Two minutes into injury time, 5ft 7in Dan James somehow beat 6ft 5in Tyrone Mings to a high ball in the box, and somehow the ball squirmed beyond Emi Martínez in the Villa goal. There was still time for Lucas Digne to miss a golden opportunity to reinstate the two-goal advantage, so both teams trudged off feeling slightly relieved and slightly annoyed at the 3-2 half-time score, while the pundits in the BT Sport studio drooled over what they described as the best half of football they'd seen all season.

The second half didn't quite live up to the same billing. Steven Gerrard would later explain that he didn't want the second half to resemble a basketball match, which struck me as odd considering Villa had scored three first-half goals under such conditions. The home side were duly punished for their conservative approach when Diego Llorente pulled Leeds level from a corner, but for the remaining 30 minutes little happened. Players were dropping like flies with cramp and injury as the frenetic first half took its toll, even on the Leeds players, and when Villa were reduced to ten men for the duration of eight minutes of injury time the Whites couldn't find the extra gear to force a winning goal, thus settling for a hard-earned point.

Despite the quiet second half, the match was roundly declared as a Premier League classic, though it irked me to hear it described as 'a great advert for English football'. It was a great advert for Bielsa's football; no other matches were anything like Bielsaball.

Everton 3 Leeds United 0

'I'm putting everything I own on Everton producing their performance of the season on Saturday.' I wish I'd followed through on my bold WhatsApp message. The Toffees came into the game on the brink of the relegation zone having suffered four straight defeats, and they'd only tasted victory once in their last 15 Premier League matches, but it was so obvious to me that the visit of Leeds would wake Everton from their mid-season slumber.

Playing Leeds always seemed to galvanise a home team, especially with Bielsa at the helm. Opponents knew they had no choice but to run their socks off for 90 minutes if they were going to compete, and their fans knew they had no choice but to sing their hearts out for 90 minutes to compete with the away following, and today there were added ingredients that created a perfect storm. Everton had just relieved themselves of the stifling atmosphere Rafa Benítez had brought to the club, replacing him with – of all people – Frank Lampard, who would undoubtably have his team fired up for his Premier League bow at Goodison Park, especially against Leeds, and his nemesis, Marcelo Bielsa.

All my fears came to fruition in a dreadful first half. Roared on by their vociferous home crowd, Everton flew out of the blocks and cut Leeds wide open within a minute, but stuttered in front of goal and the chance went begging. It mattered not. Within ten minutes the blue tidal wave had forced the ball into the net, and shortly after Rodrigo's long-range volley crashed off the bar, Michael Keane rose above Struijk to head the home side into a 2-0 lead. Another spectacular Rodrigo effort crashed off the bar before half-time, but those two near misses flattered the visitors; they had been absolutely battered.

It was such a bad performance by Leeds that it almost null-and-voided my prediction. Everton hadn't had to do anything except work hard – Leeds had done the rest with sloppy passing and slack marking, and I was so downbeat that I genuinely didn't want to watch the second half, and I wish I hadn't. Looking after a chickenpox-riddled Alessandro would have been the lesser of two evils, because in some ways the second half was even worse than the first. Everton were content with their two-goal advantage and Leeds were incapable of giving them anything to worry about as the game meandered to its inevitable finish. One wayward Dan James effort was all United could muster, and by the final whistle Everton had capped off a horrible afternoon with a deserved third goal. Bielsa accepted he had set Leeds up for failure by deploying Klich and Rodrigo in midfield, where the Whites were completely overrun, although the Twitterati were more concerned about Tyler Roberts continuing to get minutes ahead of wonderboy Joe 'Joffy' Gelhardt, not to mention El Loco's decision to withdraw an under-par Raphinha at half-time.

Perhaps if the fixture list was kinder Leeds would have still been looking upwards rather than down. With a six-point gap to 18th they were closer to the top half of the table than they were to the relegation zone, but things were bound to get hairy unless Bielsa could summon one of the biggest results of his career in the next three games. And what better game to do it in than his first taste of the War of the Roses in front of a baying Elland Road.

Leeds United 2 Manchester United 4

For every home game this season my dad had endured the abominable Leeds United ticketing website, sacrificing countless hours to get his 16-year-old grandson into Elland Road, and the one game he failed to get him a ticket for was the biggest of the lot. So he made the ultimate sacrifice and gave Lucca his ticket for 'Scum at home'.

We arrived at a sodden Elland Road, well, sodden. It was absolutely bucketing it down and Lucca's decision to wear joggers was as questionable as my decision to combat Storm Eunice with a gilet, although the most questionable decision of all came from Bielsa, as reports filtered through that Raphinha was on the bench. El Loco had been cagey in his pre-match presser, giving one-sentence answers to almost every question, but an enquiry about experiencing the Roses battle in front of an Elland Road crowd finally provoked a meaningful answer, 'The fans have always supported the team unconditionally; it's hard to imagine support beyond what we have already received. But if the presence of a classic rival increases the enthusiasm it's going to be beautiful to watch.'

The increased enthusiasm was unmistakable even half an hour before kick-off, although the booing and goading of Manchester United players throughout their pre-match warm-up wouldn't normally be described as 'beautiful'. This was cauldron Elland Road at its most hostile, and the pandemic-related protocol that prevented the teams from sharing a tunnel played right into our hands. 'The scum' were greeted with a venomous reception before the Whites were hit by a wall of noise, the likes of which we hadn't experienced for 20 years. In the early exchanges the visiting players were booed with every touch, but when they went down injured they were cheered (as if we all believed they were actually injured and not just whinging), while Cristiano Ronaldo, with over 800 career goals to his name, was left in no doubt as to what type of predator the Leeds fans believed he was.

A long stoppage due to an actual injury to Robin Koch took the edge off the atmosphere somewhat, and when the German eventually succumbed it befuddled Bielsa's team. One of the major issues with Leeds's perennial injury struggles was that most injuries were occurring during the matches themselves, and conceding within minutes of mid-game reshuffles was not uncommon. Right on cue, just three minutes after Koch was withdrawn, Harry Maguire opened the scoring, capitalising on some schoolboy marking from Llorente. There was no big response from the home side, who once again struggled to build any attacks without the Yorkshire Pirlo there to dictate, and in the 50th minute of the half the visitors scored another simple goal when Bruno Fernandes headed home unmarked from inside the six-yard box.

'They're going to have to start the second half off like a train,' tweeted Phil Hay, and Bielsa set the tone by using his final two substitutions to introduce Joe Gelhardt and Raphinha at half-time. Six minutes later, a great tackle by Firpo set Rodrigo away down the left wing, and his misjudged cross (or sensational shot) floated beyond the desperate reach of David de Gea and dropped inside the far post. Amid wild celebrations all around, Raphinha grabbed the ball from the back of the net and rushed it back to the centre circle as quickly as he could.

Straight from kick-off, Dallas dived into a tackle and regained possession to the delighted roars of the Elland Road crowd, and there was another roar as Raphinha kept the ball in play by a fraction. The Brazilian's pass infield was loose, but Elland Road was roaring again as Forshaw ploughed through Fernandes to instantly win back possession, and when Dan James drilled a cross into the corridor of uncertainty, Raphinha slid in ahead of Luke Shaw to put the ball back whence he'd retrieved it just 58 seconds earlier, the back of the net. Elland Road exploded in delirious jubilation; nobody could believe what they had just witnessed. Manchester United's two-goal lead was gone in 60 seconds!

With Leeds's players as buoyant as their fans the game was there to be won. The unrelenting rain made for treacherous conditions, and the sight of splashed water with every step and bounce, along with the uncertainty of every pass, added to a spellbinding spectacle. The Whites were flying into tackles and I was impressed that the referee was happy to let it all go as if it were the 1990s, although when it came to booking the opposition he refereed like it was the 1960s; Scott McTominay would have needed to give someone a right hook to receive a caution.

After 20 hectic minutes, the pivotal moment of the match arrived when a cross into the box had Leeds players lined up to score. The opportunity to etch his name into the history books at Elland Road fell to Dan James, but to the dismay of the Kop he barely even connected with a simple-looking header, and less than a minute later Fred found himself free in the box and beat Meslier at his near post. I felt sick with regret. Joe Gelhardt was the biggest threat as Leeds attempted another comeback, but from a couple of sniffs of goal he couldn't find the net, and in the 88th minute a mistake by Struijk was punished by Anthony Elanga, who sealed a 4-2 victory for his team. 'WE'RE LEEDS, AND WE'RE PROUD OF IT!' sang the Kop at full time, bestowing on their beaten heroes an ovation their efforts deserved. They had given everything, but it hadn't been enough.

I was drained and deflated after the game. A riveting second half, and perhaps the most spine-tingling minute I'd ever experienced at Elland Road notwithstanding, the fact Leeds had eventually capitulated weighed heavy on my mind. For all their fighting spirit, in recent weeks Bielsa's side had begun to show traits of a team that gets dragged deep into relegation trouble; they were conceding sloppy goals, losing big moments in big matches, and now had the second-worst goal difference in the Premier League. And next up was Anfield.

Liverpool 6 Leeds United 0

Having been so excited to visit Anfield on Boxing Day, by the time the rescheduled fixture came around I was dreading it. Leeds may have stood a better chance of avoiding a battering, but at least on Boxing Day we would have made a day of it, rather than rushing across the country after work, probably getting spanked, then rushing home to try and get some sleep before Alessandro woke up. That sounded no fun at all, it sounded like City revisited, which is precisely what the bookies expected as they offered the same odds for a Leeds win (14/1) as they did for a six-goal Liverpool victory. My only glimmer of hope was that Jürgen Klopp might rest players with the League Cup Final against Chelsea only four days away, but he didn't. Liverpool were at full strength, while Leeds were still without the spine of their team – Cooper, Phillips and Bamford – and tonight their Spanish and German international centre-backs, Koch and Llorente, were both missing too.

My brother Gianni, a Liverpool season ticket holder, was the big winner from the Boxing Day postponement. He had been due to move back home from Tokyo before Christmas, but Covid-related delays meant he didn't make it to England until the new year. His friend, P, had kindly let me use his ticket, so Gianni and I would be on the Kop together for the first time since 1997, when we were teenagers and went hungry all day after forgetting to take money for food. History repeated itself 25 years later as we went hungry again, although this time money wasn't the problem. We were lacking an even more precious commodity: time. Work commitments had delayed our departure and we only managed to park up at 7.30pm, giving us a decent chance of making kick-off but only if we ran to the ground. No problem for two seasoned marathon runners, you might have thought, but Gianni pulled a muscle five minutes into the run, condemning us to listen to 'You'll Never Walk Alone' from the queues at the Kop turnstile.

In the end we only missed the first minute of the match, and the next ten were encouraging. Leeds started positively and almost took the lead, but Dan James's woes continued as he stumbled with the goal at his mercy. Moments later a cross struck Dallas on the arm, the referee pointed to the spot, and Mo Salah converted with ease. Just what Leeds didn't need. The Whites responded positively and only an offside flag denied Raphinha an equaliser in front of the Kop, but moments later Joel Matip was allowed to saunter from defence to attack and double the lead. As well as Leeds had competed, they were practically dead and buried inside half an hour.

I spent the rest of the match clock-watching. All I cared about was avoiding another embarrassing pummelling, and with half-time almost upon us I was quite comfortable with what I had seen as Leeds trailed 2-0. Then Liverpool were awarded another dodgy penalty, which Salah converted again, and 3-0 at half-time felt uncomfortably ominous. Yet after the break there were no signs of impending catastrophe. Leeds continued the only way they knew how – trying to attack at every opportunity, trying to pass their way from one goal to another, and trying to retrieve every dead ball as quickly as possible – and although they failed to produce the dazzling football we saw on Bielsa's Premier League debut at Anfield, I was still proud of their determination, commitment and bravery.

The second-half resistance lasted until the 80th minute, but heading into injury time at 4-0 didn't feel like a disaster. Then disaster struck. Mané grabbed his second of the night to dampen my remaining spirit, and with the last action of the game Virgil van Dijk was left completely alone to head in a soul-crushing sixth. My heart sank. Leeds had capitulated, and such an embarrassing scoreline left no room for mitigating factors. Bielsa's name had been ringing out from the away end, but The Great Man was sure to cop both barrels from the Twitterati after this.

Watching from the Kop hadn't actually made the night any more painful. With the result never in doubt this had been like a pre-season friendly to the Kopites, although when Jürgen Klopp saluted them after the final whistle with one fist pump for each goal the Kop suddenly went wild, breaking into their loudest chant of the night, 'LIVERPOOL, LIVERPOOL!' At this point I decided to check my phone and saw a message from my old boss, Chris, sympathising with the Leeds result and apologising for his beloved Spurs losing to Burnley. That hurt more than the result. Due to the pre-match rush I hadn't even realised Burnley were playing, but they were now just three points behind Leeds with two games in hand, and a vastly superior goal difference. And to make matters worse, Spurs were next up at Elland Road and I fully expected a backlash.

Leeds United 0 Tottenham Hotspur 4

'How can I defend myself when the team has conceded the most goals in the Premier League?' El Loco was at his lowest ebb in the pre-Spurs press conference, and it was so sad to hear him talking in such a manner. 'It would be naive to think, in a moment of weakness like we are in, that faith, confidence and credibility are the same as they were. The only one who believes blindly in myself is me.'

Tell that to my 666 Twitter followers, Marcelo! On the morning after the Anfield annihilation I tweeted in defence of the team, insisting they had competed well for 80 minutes ('conceding only once, plus two daft penalties'), then spent the afternoon responding to the hordes of people who called me 'deluded', 'drunk', or 'on spice'. My tweet received 600 likes vs 100 disparaging comments, which may or may not have been representative of the feelings of the entire fanbase, but it was clear that many people believed we were approaching the end of the Bielsa era.

Perhaps in the back of my mind I sensed this too. On the morning of the Spurs match I blurted out to Frankie that this could be the biggest game of my life, but when she asked why, I couldn't bring myself to say the words, to admit that I feared Bielsa's job might be on the line. Deep down, I don't believe I really thought The Great Man could be sacked; my main concern was the reaction of the fans, not the board, to another heavy defeat. Inside Elland Road there had only ever been one murmur of dissent against Bielsa (when the faithful disagreed with a substitution against Preston in 2019, a change that saved the match), but the doubters were growing in number and volume on social media, and I hated the prospect of this negativity seeping into the stadium, causing a civil war among a fanbase that had never been so united as they were under El Loco.

There was a strangely subdued atmosphere in the Kop prior to the match, almost fearful, and the Dave to my right agreed with my meagre aspirations: to steer clear of another thrashing. Alas, by the 26th minute Leeds were 3-0 down, having allowed Spurs to score three simple goals while barely breaking sweat. It was a disaster. United had been unlucky at the other end – Struijk missed a free header at 0-0, Koch struck the inside of the post at 1-0, and Ayling put another free header over the bar at 2-0 – but even I couldn't defend this performance or even begrudge the boos that greeted the half-time whistle. It was the first time Bielsa's team had been booed off since he took the job almost four years earlier.

Tottenham took their foot off the gas in the second half, but Leeds's demoralised players just couldn't work themselves back into the game. A sign of their lack of confidence came when Hugo Lloris's uncanny Kiko Casilla impersonation presented last season's player of the year, Stuart Dallas, with an open goal. Dallas could have rolled the ball into an empty net from 25 yards but instead dribbled towards goal, not confident enough to shoot until he was six yards out, by which time the defenders had recovered ground and his shot was blocked. In the 85th minute Son Heung-min completed the scoring from Harry Kane's sublime long ball over the defence, but the Leeds players kept plugging away and clocked up a total of 19 shots, and when the final whistle blew they collapsed to the floor, devastated. Raphinha couldn't drag himself up and players from both teams consoled him, creating a scene that was barely befitting of the situation. There were still 12 games remaining and Leeds weren't even in the drop zone, but Elland Road was so sombre it reminded me of the day they were relegated from the Championship. There were no boos from the fans, just a sad resignation, and the players were clapped as they trudged apologetically around the ground.

On the way up Beeston Hill I checked the LUFC WhatsApp group and Adam had shared a screenshot of Phil Hay's article on The Athletic, titled 'Bielsa's future at Leeds in serious doubt, Marsch in line to replace him'. I was aghast, but I couldn't believe they were actually going to sack our messiah. On the journey home I tried to convince myself that it wasn't true, that the board were just testing the waters, but the writing was on the wall. When my dad dropped me off he started to tell Frankie the news that Bielsa was getting sacked, but I couldn't allow myself to hear it and practically slammed the door in his face. Frankie asked if I wanted a hug but I refused, and I now realise this was me experiencing the first stage of grief: denial. I just couldn't bring myself to acknowledge what was happening.

I spent the rest of the evening glued to Twitter as the story intensified. First talkSPORT reported that Bielsa had indeed been sacked, then Phil Hay distastefully wrote a eulogy on the Bielsa era, without confirming his departure or expanding upon the story. There was no word from the club and the fanbase was in meltdown. Despite all the debate on Twitter about Bielsa's position, now that he was about to be sacked it seemed nobody wanted it to happen. Finally, at 11pm, Hay tweeted again, confirming there would be no announcement tonight and adding, 'Let's see what the morning brings.' That was good enough for me. I could go to bed safe in the knowledge that Bielsa was still the Leeds manager. He had turned water into wine and fed the 35,000 with a loaf of bread, so perhaps he could rise from the dead.

The next morning there was still no news. Had the backlash from the fans made the club U-turn on their decision? We had a family outing planned at Harewood House and set off at 9am. Still no news. At 10am there was still no news, but at 11am I checked my phone again and at the top of my Twitter feed was the announcement that cut me to the bone: 'Leeds United can confirm the club have parted company with head coach Marcelo Bielsa.'

I was numbed by the realisation that the Bielsa era was over, walking the grounds of Harewood House like a zombie. Frankie, Alessandro and I sat on one side of a picnic table to eat our packed lunch and were soon asked by another young family if they could use the other side. They sat down and the mother was comforting her young son, telling him how much everybody would miss Bielsa. The dad was silent. I still regret not opening my mouth; unquestionably we would have all felt better sharing each other's pain, especially if I had told them the story of Bielsa coming to my house. But I couldn't face it, I wasn't ready to talk.

The Crucifixion of the Messiah

Losing El Loco hit me hard, really hard, harder than I ever expected. Being a 'widow of Bielsa' can't be easy at the best of times, but I'd never considered any scenario except Bielsa leaving of his own accord. Being sacked by the club I loved made it so much harder to accept.

To me, this was a despicable decision, and eradicated my devout support of our board. The Great Man would likely have echoed the sentiments of Jesus of Nazareth at his own crucifixion – 'Forgive them Father, for they know not what they do' – but I couldn't see myself ever forgiving them for this. I was straight into stage two of grief, experiencing an anger so fierce that part of me wanted the board punishing with relegation. They had tarnished Bielsa's legacy and he would now for ever have his philosophy questioned by people that could legitimately argue that his methods had been 'found out'.

Maybe it was true, maybe I was blinded by love, but if my love was blind my faith certainly wasn't. Bielsa had kept Leeds's heads above water even through a torrid run of fixtures without the whole spine of his team. That run was over. Leeds's next seven games were all against the Premier League's 'beatable' clubs, and Cooper, Phillips and Bamford would soon be available again. Bielsa had also suffered similar dips in form in the January and February of his previous three seasons, and each time his team had bounced back stronger than ever. Why wouldn't they do so again?

There were many fans who agreed with the decision of course, even if most who did still didn't like it. 'It's Leeds United, not Bielsa United' was a common notion on Twitter, but while no man could be bigger than the club, no manager could be better than Bielsa, and I just wanted to watch Bielsaball. I wanted to hear his pearls of wisdom each week, see photos of him in Costa and Morrisons, and have the option of driving through Wetherby, just because there was a slim chance of catching a glimpse of The Great Man in the flesh.

It was soon revealed that the board had long since decided to replace El Loco in the summer with the American coach, Jesse Marsch, a change they decided to bring forward following the defeat to Liverpool. Marsch had achieved success in the MLS with New York Red

Bulls and in Austria with Red Bull Salzburg, but his only experience in one of Europe's major leagues had lasted less than four months when he was sacked by Red Bull Leipzig following elimination from the Champions League group stage, having collected only 18 points from 14 Bundesliga matches. It was hardly an exciting CV, but the world hadn't stopped going round so what choice was there but to keep supporting the team and hope for the best?

I did wonder whether a change from man-marking to zonal may take some much-needed pressure off the players. It also stood to reason that the players would benefit from Marsch's hands-on man-management style, having gone four years with as little interaction with Bielsa as possible. Also, if Bielsa was to be replaced in the summer, then all we had really missed out on was a dozen extra games and a proper farewell. These were the most positive takes I could muster, which all had value and were a sign of me entering stage three of my grief, bargaining. Yet these feelings were all forced. Deep down I was still consumed by an anger that could only be overcome by positive results.

March 2022

Bryn Law – 'It was the end of a spectacular era, unlike any that clubs tend to experience these days. Bielsa had been incredibly successful and achieved everything he had been tasked with achieving, he'd set Leeds on a different plane to where they had been before, but it had come to an end and there was a finality about it that left you nervous about what was to come next. We'd been taken to such great heights, and there tends to be only one way to go from those heights, the inexorable slide down.'

15.	Brentford	24
16.	LEEDS	23
17.	Everton	22
18.	Burnley	21
19.	Watford	19
20.	Norwich	17

Leicester City 1 Leeds United 0

The first of March was also the first of Marsch; Jesse Marsch's first day as Leeds United manager. His opening press conference was quite uplifting. He spoke very well, came across as a likeable guy, and seemed to have a clear grasp of what he was stepping into and how to move forward. He praised the work of Bielsa and the 'fine young men' El Loco had left behind, though he did feel some of them were too nice, specifically Jack Harrison, who he wanted to become 'a son of a bitch'. Marsch also wanted to see more of Joe Gelhardt, and even for a staunch Bielsa fan it was pleasing to think we had seen the last of Dan James up front.

So, when the first post-Bielsa line-up was revealed I didn't know whether to laugh or cry. Marsch had picked the same team Bielsa would have, with Dan James still up front, but instead of playing in their natural positions, Luke Ayling covered for Robin Koch at centre-back, Koch covered for Stuart Dallas in midfield, and Dallas covered for Ayling at right-back. 'Make it make sense' as Gen Z might put it. Once the match started it was clear to see a tweak in the tactics – the marking was zonal, the midfield two of Koch and Klich were horizontal rather than vertical, and the wingers weren't as wide – which helped Leeds control play against a Leicester side who were struggling for consistency in the Premier League amid a run to the latter stages of the inaugural Europa Conference League. Juggling two competitions was an age-old problem for teams outside of the Rich Six, but Brendan Rodgers was still coming under pressure despite having won the FA Cup in the previous season. Modern football, eh?

It was a blessing that this game coincided with Adam's stag do. Gallons of beer and perennial Jägerbombs helped numb the pain of watching post-Bielsa Leeds, while still suffering the archetypal Bielsa defeat. The Whites spurned chance after chance, had two massive penalty appeals controversially waved away, and the only chance the opposition created hit the back of the net. Everything had changed but nothing had changed.

At the end of the match came the stark reality of life under a new manager, as Marsch gathered his players in a big huddle in the centre circle to deliver his post-match team talk in the glare of the world's media. It made me shudder to think what Bielsa must have made of it all, but The Great Man wouldn't have made anything of it. He was pictured walking the streets of Wetherby during the match, clearly too heartbroken to watch, and the sight of him in normal clothes rather than his Leeds tracksuit was even more upsetting than a fifth defeat on the trot.

Leeds United 0 Aston Villa 3

Oddly enough, relegation hadn't seriously crossed my mind in the aftermath of Marcelo Bielsa's sacking. I still had faith in the squad he created and believed they would pull themselves clear of trouble once the key players returned from injury, but all that changed after Jesse Marsch's first match at Elland Road.

I didn't know how I'd feel being back at Elland Road. I knew it would be strange, but I hoped seeing Leeds in the flesh, surrounded by Leeds fans, would aid my grieving process and reignite the doused fire in my belly. My feelings of detachment weren't helped by a sombre and subdued atmosphere in the Kop, which only intensified due to a bewildering display by the home team. They were clueless in possession and confused out of possession, and even before Coutinho gave Villa a 22nd-minute lead my dad had compared the performance to League One Leeds (the Dennis Wise version; Simon Grayson's talented team was much better than this, as was Gary McAllister's).

A 1-0 half-time deficit was flattering for the hosts, but the interval brought an opportunity for Marsch to whip his boys into shape. Alarmingly, after the break things only got worse. Leeds couldn't lay a glove on their opponents, and the players looked completely dejected as they continued to hoof long balls over the top of a defence that was far too wily to succumb to such basic tactics. I couldn't be sure whether the players were under instruction to play such archaic, route-one football, but it was clear Marsch's preferred 4-2-2-2 'Penis Formation' was not working at all, while the zonal marking seemed to have the players' heads in a spin – they were in disarray. The board had insisted the new manager would provide a seamless progression from Bielsaball but on this showing his tactics were the polar opposite.

By the 70th minute Leeds were 3-0 down and the home fans could no longer control their frustrations, airing their disapproval in the name of El Loco as chants of 'MAAARCELO BIELSA!' rang around the ground. The protestation wasn't aimed at the new manager but the 'holy trinity' of Andrea Radrizzani, Victor Orta and Angus Kinnear, who had dropped a bomb on the club by sacking the biggest asset they had. With Elland Road as toxic as it had been for many years I felt on the verge of tears.

All the love and harmony of the Bielsa era was gone. It felt like we'd been transported back to the most rotten times and now I wasn't just fearing relegation – it suddenly felt inevitable.

More boos rang around Elland Road as the home team stood off the Aston Villa defence in the closing stages, allowing them to knock the ball around unchallenged. This was the last thing the fans wanted to see, a red rag to an angry and emotional bull, and Elland Road was booing again as the final whistle signalled a club record-equalling sixth straight league defeat. Sections of the Kop even booed the players during their lap of appreciation, or perhaps these boos were aimed at Jesse Marsch, who had joined the players on the pitch. I almost raised a smile at the thought of Marsch gathering the players for another post-match huddle – the Kop's reaction would have been priceless – but disappointingly he refrained.

As I walked back up Beeston Hill, I contemplated everything I'd witnessed in 30 years of watching Leeds United and concluded that tonight had been among the saddest occasions I'd ever seen at Elland Road. The hope and belief that Leeds were going to realise their full potential under El Loco's guidance was gone, and all we had left was a group of demoralised players and an inexperienced manager, who had somehow charmed Orta and Radrizzani into believing he was better suited for the job than the man who had single-handedly turned their football club around, the man the players owed their whole careers to. In my despair I was convinced Leeds were doomed. I couldn't see them getting another win, or even another point.

Leeds United 2 Norwich City 1

In Marcelo Bielsa's final press conference he had delivered the gut-wrenching news that Patrick Bamford still couldn't run and would remain unavailable for the foreseeable future, while in Jesse Marsch's first press conference he'd pledged to allow the players more recovery time in order to stem the tide of injuries. That being the case, I was perplexed when Bamford was named on the bench for Marsch's first match at Leicester, and after playing 15

Saluting the champions at Blackburn

Ayling's Old Trafford stunner

Saluting the champions at Elland Road

Sent James' Park, pet

Lad 'n Dad

Come on you Lilacs

Barely room for his bucket, let alone 13 steps

In 'the Gods'

Before the bad stuff happened

7-0 and still singing

Holding the hand of the team

Friends Re-United

Mind the gap

Probably better than Upton Park

Bielsa's Circle of Trust

Greeting the Scum

A horrible night on the Kop

Contemplating the worst

Drowning our sorrows

A Brighter Day

The show must go on

Footage from the secret away end

The sun sets on our Premier League adventure

Elation after Joffy's miracle

Safe

minutes against Aston Villa he was back in the starting line-up for the visit of Norwich.

Whatever the truth of the Bamford situation, there was no hiding from the decision to leave an injured and immobilised Tyler Roberts on the pitch for the last 15 minutes at Leicester. According to Marsch, the Welshman had been insistent on finishing the game, and now he was ruled out for the rest of the season. The injury hoodoo that had plagued the season continued when Junior Firpo was carried off against Aston Villa, but losing the only specialist left-back at the club at least meant there would be no choice but to reinstate Luke Ayling at right-back, with the current incumbent, Stuart Dallas, the only solution at left-back. Hence, the line-up for this critical, must-win match against rock-bottom Norwich looked perfectly balanced. Diego Llorente was fit to partner Pascal Struijk in defence, Klich and Forshaw were two natural midfielders in midfield, Bamford a natural striker up front, while Koch, Harrison and Gelhardt provided quality options from the bench. It was as strong a line-up as Leeds had fielded all season, against the very opponent Marsch would have hand-picked to follow his nightmare introduction to Elland Road. Nevertheless, the easiest fixture on the calendar came at a price; Leeds were under immense pressure not only to win, but to deliver a performance that would restore belief in the team and generate faith in the new coach.

Despite being such a vital match I still felt empty inside as I took my place in the Kop, though it was pleasing to see Leeds start well. Everything that didn't work during that godforsaken Thursday night against Aston Villa was working this time: Raphinha and James were enjoying acres of space when drifting inside, Rodrigo was pulling the strings like prime Pablo Hernández, and the opening goal stemmed from a hopeful long punt towards the penalty spot. It was Rodrigo who feasted on the spoils, but there were no limbs in the Kop from me, only laughter at the fact Marsch's route-one approach had actually paid off. Meanwhile, the Norwich players were furious that the goal wasn't ruled out for offside, especially goalkeeper Tim Krul, who chased the referee around the pitch complaining to no avail. Bamford had been offside, but having made no attempt to play the ball he was judged to be not interfering, even though his presence forced the defender to deal with an otherwise harmless ball. It was the wrong decision in the spirit of the game but correct by the letter of the stupidly overcomplicated offside law, which had tied itself in knots since the introduction of VAR (as had the handball rule).

It was an excellent first-half display by Leeds; they really should have been out of sight, and much of their good work was enabled due to Patrick Bamford's superb display leading the line. Unfortunately, Bamford had given all he could and for the second half it was back to Dan James up front. Nevertheless, the Whites continued to dominate until the hour, when the impressive Mateusz Klich was replaced by Robin Koch. This defensive reinforcement bemused and exasperated me in equal measure. How could Marsch relent against the worst team in the league with so long to go, in a match Leeds were completely bossing?

Having offered no threat all afternoon, Norwich duly took control. There was a lucky escape when a long-range drive thundered off Meslier's bar, but no sooner had the bar stopped shaking than the visitors were awarded a penalty following Luke Ayling's dangerous lunge in the box. After a long pause it became clear that the decision was being reviewed by VAR, but because there had been no complaints from Ayling I was stunned when the referee was summoned to the pitchside monitor. The Norwich players were furious at the inevitable reversal of the decision, and the official had to turn back and deal with the ensuing fracas before consulting the technology. Three excruciating minutes after the penalty was awarded, the decision was finally reversed because the attacker had trod on Ayling's foot rather than been tripped by it. United had been rescued twice in one game by the stupid rules and VAR, and my imagination played out the image of Bielsa spending all season filling a fruit machine with pound coins, only for Marsch to scoop the jackpot on his third spin!

The Football Gods were in frivolous mood, however, and after Raphinha hit the bar with another brilliant free kick, Norwich scored a gut-churning equaliser on the stroke of 90 minutes, a goal that horrified Elland Road. There was no anger from the terraces, just utter dejection, and a unanimous acceptance that Leeds were going down.

Before Jesse Marsch could even react, Joe Gelhardt was stripped off and ready to come on. Two minutes later he took to the pitch, and in the 94th minute the 5ft 10in teenager leapt like a salmon to beat Ben Gibson to a long Meslier clearance he had no right to win, flicking the ball on towards Raphinha, who reached it just before the defender and found himself clean through on goal. The Brazilian shaped to shoot but rounded the goalkeeper instead, and although his touch took him too wide to score, his awareness, temperament and elegance enabled him to cut the ball back, perfectly into the path of the arriving Gelhardt, who converted into an empty net to send Elland Road into an ecstatic fit of pandemonium. It was almost unbelievable. Somehow Leeds had saved themselves, somehow they had dug out an imperative victory, and while all around me were having out-of-body experiences, I could only watch and hold back the tears, for what, I didn't know. They certainly weren't tears of joy, they can't have been tears of sorrow, and I don't think tears of relief is a thing. I felt like I had just witnessed a divine intervention, as if the goal had been scored from above, or from Rosario.

If God was the one responsible for this victory, his work was not done yet. One of the craziest halves of football I had ever witnessed was seconds from completion when a half-cleared corner fell to Norwich keeper Krul on the edge of the Leeds box. With a feather touch his countryman Dennis Bergkamp would have been proud of, Krul split the Leeds defence, but with the goal at his mercy Teemu Pukki's finish hit Meslier square in the face and the ball was scrambled to safety. With that the game was won. Leeds United had been given a huge shot in the arm – their survival bid was up and running.

After the game I felt like the only Leeds fan not bouncing off the walls. I'd just seen a goal so seismic that it could alter the landscape at Elland Road for a generation, yet I only felt regretful, because Marcelo Bielsa wasn't there to see it. I was shocked, annoyed, worried and ashamed that I'd not been able to enjoy such a historic moment. I was entering stage four of my grief, depression.

Wolverhampton Wanderers 2 Leeds United 3

My Bielsa grief had denied me the euphoria of Joffy's magical winning goal, but it didn't spoil my enjoyment of the footage that emerged online in the aftermath. The goal accompanied by Bryn Law's commentary was just brilliant, with his screams of joy cutting short his fears that Raphinha had taken the ball too wide to score, and his concluding line the work of a maestro, so simple and poignant, 'GELHARDT *IS* THE HERO!'

The best footage was filmed by a pitchside camera that was purely fixed on Leeds's technical area from the South Stand. It showed the substitutes all standing up like meerkats (in unison with the fans behind them) when Raphinha raced clear, then running into the technical area and stopping like racehorses on the start line as Rapha rounded the keeper, before sprinting in jubilation to mob Joffy by the corner flag as the fans in the West Stand went crazy. What a sight to behold, and the audio was glorious too; the collective 'GO ON!' of the crowd, then silence, then another 'GO ON!', before silence again, and finally an explosion of noise when the ball hit the net. What a sport football can be, even without Bielsa.

'Benchcam' went viral with millions of views from all around the world (Elland Road's poshest stand subsequently won Twitter's unofficial 'Limbs of the Season' award) and a week of watching this uplifting footage over and over helped my mood. By Friday I was actually excited about the evening's match at Wolves, which would be watched in the pub with my mates. I was intrigued to see whether the tactics that worked so well in the first hour against Norwich could work against a proper Premier League team, one that was having a great campaign and hopeful of qualifying for Europe for the third time in four seasons.

The tactics did work, until the 23rd minute, when Patrick Bamford pulled up with a recurrence of his injury and was immediately substituted (so much for not rushing players back, Jesse!). Three minutes later Wolves opened the scoring, and the pain of conceding was magnified by the sight of Bamford sat on the bench with tears in his eyes, and the sympathetic arm of captain Liam Cooper around his shoulder. His season was clearly over, and Leeds's had taken another nosedive.

In my post-Bielsa slump, scoring goals may not have stirred the emotions but conceding them certainly did, especially when they came in the 56th minute of a first half. All my pent-up emotions were released as I screamed bloody murder at our sleeping defence, after a quick free kick caught them cold and allowed Wolves to double their lead. It had been a disaster of a half. Leeds were 2-0 down, Bamford was crocked, and Diego Llorente and Mateusz Klich had both been forced off too, and, incredibly, just five minutes into the second half Leeds suffered a fourth injury when Raúl Jiménez clattered into Illan Meslier. Fortunately (and I use that term very loosely), Klich's injury had counted as a 'concussion substitution', so the Whites were allowed to use a fourth substitute and handed a debut to 21-year-old goalkeeper Kristoffer Klaesson. The genuinely good news was a second yellow card shown to Jiménez, but I didn't have any hope of saving the game, not against a Wolves side who were masters in the dark arts of time-wasting, and boasted the fourth-best defensive record in the country.

A factor in the decision to sack Bielsa may have been the incessant injuries, but following his dismissal the rate of injuries was somehow accelerating and United's side now resembled the sort they would field in a League Cup second round tie, with Meslier, Cooper, Llorente, Firpo, Phillips, Klich, Raphinha and Bamford all absent, plus Roberts, Shackleton and Gelhardt for good measure. Nevertheless, the remaining players stepped up to the plate and within ten minutes they were back in the game thanks to a scrappy goal from Jack Harrison. Three minutes later, they equalised thanks to a scrappy goal from Rodrigo and the pub erupted, though I only allowed myself a solitary yelp of approval. It was now all to play for but I wasn't getting swept up in the emotion of it all, and even when Luke Ayling lashed in another scrappy goal to complete a stunning comeback in the 91st minute, I just couldn't let loose. A reflex reaction forced me to jump and shout when the ball hit the net, but in the next moment I was reduced to observer again as everybody around me went doolally.

I may have lost the ability to experience positive emotions, but I was still awash with nerves until the 100th minute when the full-time whistle finally blew. Leeds had recorded back-to-back miraculous wins, earning six points that were as important as they were dramatic, and the significance of receiving such huge morale boosts when the club was on its knees made this week incomparable to any other in my 30 years of supporting Leeds United – never had the Football Gods shined on the club so favourably. Yet I had taken no joy from it, and the fact I was missing out on such euphoric highs plunged me deeper into depression. I was still so bitter about Bielsa's sacking and felt ashamed of myself for being a bad Leeds fan, and ashamed for getting so down over something so trivial (relative to other mental health triggers). I also felt sorry for myself for having these feelings in the first place, and all these emotions manifested in a vicious cycle.

We had arranged to record the *Leeds, That* podcast straight after the game, which gave me the perfect alibi to bail on the post-match celebrations. In the darkest times this season – even after El Loco's sacking – chatting to Paul and James on the podcast had always helped, but tonight I felt too low and couldn't face trying to disguise my plight, or opening up and killing what was sure to be an ecstatic vibe. Did I love Bielsa more than Leeds United? Of course I didn't. But then why was I not over the moon and jumping for joy? Was football over for me for ever? If these two victories couldn't pull me out of my stupid stupor, what could? Only time, I hoped.

April 2022

Bryn Law – 'I spoke to Jesse on the day he arrived at the club, and while we were doing the interview he was fully aware that fans were gathering outside Thorp Arch, waiting to see off Bielsa. When does that ever happen, that you arrive at a football club that's in trouble, and the supporters are cheering the sacked manager as he departs?'

15.	Brentford	30
16.	LEEDS	29
17.	Everton	25
18.	Watford	22
19.	Burnley	21
20.	Norwich	17

Leeds United 1 Southampton 1

Like the Norwich match, I got my enjoyment from the extraordinary victory at Wolves in the aftermath. The following day I rewatched the second half and marvelled at a heroic performance. With the Whites chasing the game at 100mph it was just like watching Bielsaball, and it was thanks to Bielsa's close integration of the senior and development squads that the youngsters with almost no experience – Klaesson, Cresswell and Greenwood –

could slot into the team so seamlessly. It gave me a new perspective. This was still El Loco's team, just with a different man at the helm, and they had to stay up to preserve The Great Man's legacy. Watching the players celebrating so passionately with the fans also made me realise that Premier League football was on the line for them as well, and they deserved to remain Premier League players for their unmitigated commitment to getting Leeds there in the first place. I still loved them, and their legacies needed protecting too.

So heading into April I was feeling much better, and the Premier League table was looking much better too. Burnley still had enough games in hand to overturn the eight-point gap to United, but having only won three times all season the idea of them winning all three outstanding fixtures seemed preposterous. Therefore, with a victory over Southampton, who were sitting pretty on 35 points and coasting to safety, Leeds would be on the verge of coasting to safety themselves. The Saints were managed by another 'Red Bull guy' in Ralph Hasenhüttl, an Austrian who shared the same philosophy as Jesse Marsch and was a fellow disciple of Ralf Rangnick (whose tactics were plunging Manchester United to new lows). Interestingly, Hasenhüttl had previously described himself as 'the opposite of Bielsa', which begged the question, 'Was Marsch really a natural progression from Bielsaball?' Answers on a postcard please, Victor!

With both teams playing the same narrow system it was little surprise they cancelled each other out, but they shouldn't have done. Leeds were very good in the opening stages, with Raphinha excelling in a more central role, having become increasingly isolated in the final weeks of Bielsa's reign. Rodrigo's form had also improved post-Bielsa, and the record signing was creator-in-chief as United tore into the visitors. The high-octane performance had me feeling positive about the future under Marsch, but once Jack Harrison poked Leeds ahead the Whites went into their shells, and chances thereafter were few and far between. Southampton eventually equalised in the second half with a trademark set piece from James Ward-Prowse, whose 25-yard curler into the top corner left Meslier with no chance. I knew it was in from the moment the bloke behind me said, 'It's too close for him to get it up and down.'

Although it was frustrating to see Leeds settle for a draw, the 1-1 stalemate took them a point closer to their ultimate goal, plus, both Liam Cooper and Kalvin Phillips had completed successful comebacks after three months on the sidelines. The return of these influential players was a huge boost for everyone at Elland Road, but even so, the Whites had missed a golden opportunity to pull clear of danger, and the next match against 18th-placed Watford now became critical.

Watford 0 Leeds United 3

The Bielsa card I often played in order to gain approval to attend away games had expired, but the relegation card was a joker up my sleeve and Frankie kindly allowed me to attend what might have been my last Premier League away game for who knows how long. George had managed to get tickets in the secret away end and we met at King's Cross, enjoying a hat-trick of pints in the bright London sunshine before our onward journey to Watford. The local

Wetherspoon pub was packed out with boisterous Leeds fans, who left us rueful of the fact we wouldn't be spending the whole afternoon with them, although our tickets in the Elton John Stand were the next best thing. We were sat right in front of the away end, low down on the bottom row, with a terrible view of the pitch but the perfect spot for observing the travelling army.

The Leeds supporters were in fine voice, singing relentlessly as their team partook in a scrappy game of little quality. There was plenty of running around and plenty of endeavour, but no periods of dominance despite Watford looking like a side already doomed to relegation. The Watford fans, having been subjected to eight successive home defeats, seemed to have accepted their fate and gave little to no encouragement to their plodding team, who played with a modicum of hope but no belief.

A 20-yard Raphinha shot flew in off the near post to give the visitors a first-half lead, and in the second half Watford should have drawn level but blazed a clear chance high over the bar. If that miss didn't tell the story of why Roy Hodgson's Hornets were going down, Leeds's next goal did. It came from calamitously clumsy defending by both centre-halves, who somehow fumbled the ball between them, allowing Rodrigo to pounce, skip round the keeper, and fire into the net. The Leeds fans were loving it, and George and I loved watching the blissful scenes. The victory was sealed by a Jack Harrison thunderbolt from the edge of the box, a shot that flew as straight as an arrow into the far corner. I couldn't help leaping out of my seat at the sight of such a beautiful goal, the first time I'd ever lost control in a secret away end. Leeds were home and hosed.

'OH, O-O-O-OH, O-O-O-OH, RODRIGO MOREEENO!' The travelling army belted out their new favourite chant on repeat for the rest of the match, and when the referee blew the final whistle me and George blew our cover once and for all, joining in with the chants fervently. As we did, so did everyone around us! No wonder Watford had received such little support; we were surrounded by secret Leeds fans! The Rodrigo chant continued all the way back to King's Cross, where George and I parted ways after a celebratory Five Guys.

It had been a lovely away day, almost 18 years to the day since I last saw Leeds win away in the Premier League, and I was feeling happy for the first time since Bielsa's sacking. It hadn't been a great performance – Leeds's passing stats were their worst of the season – but it had been effective enough to raise questions about whether United were already safe. They weren't safe, and with 16 days off and numerous games for our rivals in between, only when Leeds next took the pitch would they know what shape they were really in.

Crystal Palace 0 Leeds United 0

The 16-day break started perfectly, with rock-bottom Norwich getting a 2-0 win against Burnley, who subsequently sacked their manager, Sean Dyche, after a decade at the helm which included two promotions, seven Premier League campaigns, and the club's first European adventure in half a century. Surely losing their figurehead was the last nail in Burnley's coffin? Not quite. The following week they picked up an impressive seven points from games against West Ham, Southampton and Wolves.

Shit had got real. Burnley were out of the bottom three and just two points behind Leeds, with 'Frank Lampard's Everton' the new occupants of the final relegation spot, sitting four points behind Leeds. With only six games remaining United were in a strong position, but their next three fixtures were against Manchester City, Arsenal and Chelsea, so it felt imperative to pick up a positive result from the Monday night trip to Selhurst Park.

Most Leeds fans were nervous about the game but I felt relaxed about our Premier League status. Part of this could be attributed to my post-Bielsa numbness, but I was also perceiving benefits from Jesse Marsch's fresh approach. The set-piece defending was better organised, the defence in general seemed more robust, and I was more encouraged than I thought I'd be by the use of 'inverted wingers'. If Leeds were to play well and win this game, it would be a big step forward in the grieving process.

It didn't come to pass. Nothing came to pass from Leeds; they couldn't pass, treating the ball like a hot potato as the game quickly descended into a turgid affair. For the second half Marsch replaced the attacking threat of Klich with the defensive-minded Koch, and whether his plan was to eke out a 0-0 draw or not, his team showed little ambition and failed to create a single chance. For the last ten minutes their backs were firmly against the wall, but a dogged defence held on for a second successive clean sheet and United had secured another point towards safety. They had also missed another opportunity to turn a three-horse relegation battle into two.

Despite a decent points haul I was still unsure about Jesse March. I wasn't a fan of how many interviews he gave, and the more I heard from him the more I detected hot air and noticed contradictions. One might diagnose these feelings as classic 'stepfather syndrome', but it was natural to be suspicious of the man who convinced Victor Orta to give him Bielsa's job despite very modest credentials. Marsch liked talking the talk, but the jury was still out on whether he could walk the walk.

My opinion of Marsch plummeted when he blamed Bielsa's training methods for the never-ending injury curse that had blighted the season. Whether true or not, it wasn't a great decision to bad-mouth The Great Man, and an angry reaction from the Twitterati forced Marsch into a poor attempt at back-tracking in his next press conference. His task was further complicated because he also had to break the news that Adam Forshaw had suffered a broken kneecap in training. Forshaw was the fourth player to be ruled out for the season since Marsch took over, and that number would rise to seven over the next three games.

Leeds United 0 Manchester City 4

I had booked a long weekend away with Frankie to celebrate the ten-year anniversary of us meeting, in blind hope that the Manchester City game would be moved to the Sunday. I was right to presume it would be televised, but it was given the Saturday evening slot and I would have to track it from Amsterdam airport. In truth, I wasn't too bothered. I'd seen quite enough Manchester City goals on my trip to the Etihad earlier in the season and Jesse Marsch may have felt the same, having seen his Leipzig side hit for six in the Champions League group stages earlier in the season (they had now reached the German cup final, had one foot in the Europa League final, and had taken 36 points from 17 league games since Marsch was sacked ... 'You're not my real dad!').

Marsch's attempts at damage limitation led him to name seven defenders in the starting 11 at Elland Road, but – and I'm running out of ways to write about this – unfathomably, the injury curse struck again when Liam Cooper pulled up in the warm-up and would be unable to feature. Losing our captain was still less distressing than the news coming from Vicarage Road, where Burnley had scored two late goals to defeat Watford 2-1 and overtake Leeds in the table. Everton still trailed the Whites by five points, but my brain was unable to compute the idea of the Toffees being relegated, so I was once again fearing for our Premier League lives.

A long delay to the first leg of our journey home meant I would be airborne for the first half, and when I landed at Schiphol airport Leeds were predictably 2-0 down. Worse still (and I've run out of ways to write about this), unfathomably, the injury curse had struck again when a horrific collision with Jack Grealish left Stuart Dallas with a broken femur. The femur is your thigh bone, the strongest bone in the human body, and to break it requires an impact so severe that you would only expect to see such an injury sustained in a car crash (or a scooter crash in my dad's case). As such, no professional from these shores had broken their femur since Leeds captain Bobby Collins in 1966 (a year before my dad did his). Dallas, a consummate professional who had started 120 of Leeds's last 121 league games, would miss the rest of this season and most of the next – heartbreaking news, and another hammer blow to the club's chances of survival.

In the end Leeds fell to a comfortable 4-0 defeat, after which Jesse Marsch paraded around Elland Road with his players, cheerleading the crowd who had been chanting incessantly through the final minutes and continued to do so. Marsch pumped his fists before holding his arms aloft as he walked down the tunnel, as if he had just become the heavyweight champion of the world. His enthusiasm knew no bounds, and in the post-match press conference Marsch claimed the 4-0 battering had 'felt like a win'.

The following day, Everton pulled off an unlikely 1-0 victory against Chelsea and now trailed Leeds by just two points, with a game in hand too. Once again it felt like the writing was on the wall. As Leeds were hitting the buffers their rivals were hitting purple patches, and it was abundantly clear that other results would not save the Whites. They would have to save themselves.

May 2022

Bryn Law – 'I didn't want to commentate on a team getting relegated. It's not only that Leeds wouldn't be playing at the highest level but also all the stuff that goes along with it, the implications for the people that work at the club. The inbuilt emotional football damage always pushes me to pessimism, and I was extremely trepidatious in terms of the outcome. It just felt like it was only going one way.'

15.	Southampton	40
16.	Burnley	34
17.	LEEDS	34
18.	Everton	32
19.	Watford	22
20.	Norwich	21

Arsenal 2 Leeds United 1

Three days before this fixture came the anniversary of Mark Viduka's stunning late goal that secured a 3-2 victory at Highbury and Leeds United's Premier League status on the penultimate weekend of the 2002/03 season. Could history repeat itself 19 years on? More likely was a repeat of the 5-0 stuffing United suffered at Highbury on the way to relegation the following season. Two days before this fixture came another nice anniversary, marking half a century since Leeds's 1-0 victory over Arsenal in the centenary FA Cup Final. Another omen that suggested we would register a famous win? I still couldn't believe it, though my hopes were raised when Mikel Arteta was awarded a new contract on the same day. His Arsenal team had Champions League qualification in their hands but a young and inexperienced side could freeze with the finishing line in their sights, and having signed a new contract it would be typical of the Football Gods to slam a custard pie in Arsenal's face.

One day before this fixture new life was breathed into Leeds United's season as Burnley crashed to a 3-1 defeat at home to Aston Villa. This one result transformed my outlook. I had been dreading the week ahead, expecting to be relegated after the final home match against Brighton the following Sunday, but now it was mathematically possible for Leeds to secure their safety that same day.

On the day of this fixture I suffered my first bout of relegation race insomnia, and I'd never been happier to be wide awake from 2am! Mourning the loss of Marcelo Bielsa had numbed me for two months but the fire in my belly was ablaze once more, and it was blazing with fury when Leeds found themselves 2-0 down after ten minutes at the Emirates. After 20 minutes they were a man down too. Luke Ayling, so often the one to pull his team-mates over the line in adversity, flew into a needless, mindless, and reckless two-footed lunge by the corner flag, and VAR correctly corrected the referee's initial decision to only book our stand-in captain. As angry as I was with Ayling I couldn't help feeling terribly sorry for him. This was his 500th league appearance, coming against the club that rejected him as a youngster, and he must have been devastated at letting everybody down, especially while wearing the captain's armband. An automatic three-match suspension ended his season there and then; was his Premier League career over too?

With credit to Jesse Marsch, his alterations to the team helped stem the tide, and a game that may well have been lost by a landslide remained in the balance to the end. The trade-off for defensive 'solidity' (inverted commas because Arsenal still registered 19 shots) was total incompetence going forward, yet in the 66th minute Leeds scored with their first attempt on goal, which came from their first corner, and their first touch inside the Arsenal box. Remarkably United should have equalised too, but in the last seconds of the game Rodrigo failed to connect properly with a six-yard header and glanced the ball safely into the goalkeeper's gloves.

To significantly compound a torrid afternoon, Everton claimed an unlikely 2-1 victory at Leicester that plunged the Whites into the relegation zone for the first time in seven months, and with just three games remaining they were staring down the barrel. It now seemed a straight shoot-out with Burnley, and I pinned my hopes on the Clarets losing their remaining fixtures: Tottenham away, Aston Villa away and Newcastle at home. If they did, Leeds would just need to eke out a single point from their remaining fixtures: Chelsea at home, Brighton at home and Brentford away, where they hadn't won for 72 years.

Leeds United 0 Chelsea 3

Leeds United were relegated at the end of Roman Abramovich's first season as owner of Chelsea, and now they were odds on to be relegated at the end of his last. Even still, the situation at Elland Road seemed fairly tranquil compared to the goings on at Stamford Bridge since Abramovich's close friend, Vladimir Putin, had led Russia into an abominable invasion of Ukraine. The response from the West was to cut Russia off, imposing sanctions on them and their closest allies. That wasn't much help to the Ukrainians though, who were left to fend for themselves against the onslaught from their psychotic neighbours, with only social media prayers and empty gestures to comfort them as their homes, hospitals and cities were obliterated. With all his assets frozen, Abramovich had no choice but to sell the club he had bought for £80m from Ken Bates, and after 19 trophies in 19 years he was now selling for over £4bn. Not a bad little venture.

Abramovich was leaving Chelsea as reigning world club champions, but they had endured a very disappointing season. Thomas Tuchel's side were already out of the title race when the trouble in Ukraine kicked off, and since then they had only registered two wins in seven league games, lost the League Cup Final, and been knocked out of the Champions League. Abramovich still had the chance to win a 20th trophy though, and the good news for Leeds was that Chelsea's FA Cup Final against Liverpool was just three days after this clash at Elland Road. The bad news was Chelsea's abysmal form meant they still needed four points to secure Champions League qualification, and Tuchel picked his strongest team.

Now that Leeds were in the bottom three I was intrigued to see whether Marsch would let them off the leash and go for broke against Chelsea. Deep down I knew the answer and expected another humbling defeat, but I was still hugely excited for a humongous match and the occasion of hosting our second-bitterest domestic rivals. It had taken ten weeks, but the post-Bielsa numbness had truly dissipated. Had time lived up to its reputation as a great healer, or was it simply the realisation that Leeds were actually going down if they didn't start picking up points? I suspect it was mainly the latter, combined with my desperation that Marcelo Bielsa's tenure would not be in vain. El Loco came to deliver us from the clutches of the EFL and re-establish Leeds United as a Premier League force; that was still achievable, and achieving it was surely the key to overcoming my grief.

It was a beautiful summer's evening in Beeston, and fish and chips were washed down by a quick pint with the Woollard brothers at the Batty bar outside the Kop. Sadly, it was all downhill within minutes of venturing inside. 'Lukaku will score after three minutes,' said my usually optimistic dad at kick-off, and how wrong he was when after three minutes it was Mason Mount who curled in the opening goal. For the second game running Leeds had failed to hold out for five minutes, and they even repeated the mindless red card halfway through the first half to effectively kill the game dead. The offender this time was Dan James, whose overzealous tackle ended Mateo Kovačić's evening and James's own season, and led Marsch to wonder in his post-match press conference whether he had 'over-motivated' the players.

Leeds went on to lose the game with a whimper, 3-0, which, on the face of it, was a result you could simply shrug your shoulders at. Yet the performance had been so inept that a 12-year-old in the East Stand likened it to 'watching someone playing *FIFA* for the first time, who doesn't know which buttons to press'. Marsch's line-up hadn't helped the situation. He'd fielded four centre-backs, with Struijk as left wing-back and Raphinha – the new star of Brazil's World Cup team, our top scorer, and best and most creative player – at right wing-back, where his most potent threat was taking long throws. If Raphinha actually had a long throw this may not have been so demeaning, but the superstar could barely reach the penalty box.

Even more damaging than removing the threat of Raphinha was taking Kalvin Phillips out of the Kalvin Phillips role in front of the defence. This eradicated Leeds's ability to play out from the back, and it didn't help that Phillips was partnered in midfield not by Polish international Klich, but teenager Lewis Bate, a player tonight's opponents had cast aside 12 months earlier, who wasn't considered good enough to even train with the Leeds first team six months earlier. Bate tried his best but it was a cruel game to throw him into. He was a little boy up against players who had won world and European titles with both club and country.

The manner of the defeat took away my last ounce of hope. Worse than the performance was the sight of Leeds's former warriors looking so disillusioned and demoralised. In a season when everything that could go wrong had gone wrong, all that was left was for the fat lady to sing, and I fully expected to hear her voice on the penultimate afternoon of the season.

Leeds United 1 Brighton & Hove Albion 1

It had reached the point where a 4am wake-up was a bit of a win, and while I waited for Alessandro to join me in the land of the living I discovered an amazing coincidence on Twitter. Today was the anniversary of a home match with Brighton on the penultimate weekend of the 1981/82 season, when a defeat would have relegated the Whites. Trailing 1-0 in the dying embers, Leeds pulled off a miraculous turnaround to snatch a 2-1 victory that lifted them out of the relegation zone heading into the final day. What I'd give for a repeat 40 years on.

It promised to be a monumental afternoon in the race for survival, with Burnley playing at midday, Leeds playing at 2pm, and Everton playing at 4.30pm. Just two points separated the teams and Burnley and Everton each had a game in hand on Leeds, and a far superior goal difference. My dad picked me up as Burnley kicked off at Tottenham, and as we approached our parking spot Harry Kane tucked away a penalty in first-half stoppage time. More good news followed on the walk to the ground, with Marsch selecting the very team I wanted him to, including Joe Gelhardt up front. It was the team El Loco would have picked too (except Koch was at right-back instead of Shackleton) and I prayed that the coach had swallowed his pride and would let the players play the way that suited them, with Phillips in his natural role and Harrison and Raphinha properly on the wings. Was it really too much to ask?

Confirmation of Burnley's defeat filtered through as the match kicked off, so if Leeds could avoid defeat they would be out of the bottom three and all the pressure would be heaped back on the Clarets. The good times kept rolling as Leeds raced out of the blocks (it's been a while since I wrote that) in a formation akin to Bielsaball, with Phillips deeper than Klich and Raphinha hogging the touchline. Harrison was still playing as an inverted winger, and I wondered whether this was a 'halfway house' following tough negotiations with the players. United should have taken an early lead after the goalkeeper fumbled a corner, but Gelhardt's hooked finish deflected to safety off Liam Cooper's head before it could cross the line, the sixth time in four seasons a Leeds player had denied his team a certain goal in such a manner.

For the rest of the half it was men against boys. Brighton – on the verge of the highest finish in their 120-year history, and fresh from thrashing Manchester United 4-0 – were undoubtedly a good team, but it wasn't their brilliance, nor their yellow shirts and blue shorts, that made them look like Brazil – it was Leeds's total disarray. Even if they were set up like the good old days, the home side could find no rhythm in possession, and 'against the ball' (as Marsch liked to put it) they were shambolic. Brighton cut through the zonal marking system with as much ease as Manchester City and Liverpool had exploited the man-marking system, but thanks to Illan Meslier and some wayward finishing Leeds headed into the break only one goal behind.

Marsch had a lot of work to do at half-time. After the game he said he could see in the players' eyes that some of them didn't believe they could turn it around, this despite his concentrated efforts on instilling belief into the squad. Earlier in the week he'd gone full David Brent, explaining how he had 'hundreds' of motivational quotes – from the likes of Muhammad Ali, John F. Kennedy, Mahatma Gandhi and Mother Teresa – that he would use to inspire the players on a regular basis. 'I love quotes,' said Marsch. 'The key is understanding what messages to use at the right time.' On this occasion Marsch ignored his vast repertoire and simply told his players, 'You must have no doubts.' His rousing words did the trick, though Leeds's vast improvement after the break may have been aided by Brighton's determination to protect what they had rather than put their hosts to the sword. Graham Potter later boasted that his side had 'upheld the integrity of the competition' with their performance, which was absolutely true. Despite having nothing to play for they still feigned injury at every opportunity, no matter how innocuous the incident (the ball hitting a player in the leg led to one such 'injury'). Sadly, that is what was expected in professional football, and now there was no Bielsa to teach people the errors of their ways.

The hosts had a host of chances to equalise as they poured towards a desperate Kop end, with Raphinha coming closest when sliding to meet Rodrigo's majestic ball, but only making enough contact to steer it agonisingly wide of the post. The most glaring miss came from Klich, who fired straight at the keeper from eight yards, and when the influential Pole was substituted in the 83rd minute it sparked derision from the terraces and became the moment Elland Road finally let their feelings be known. 'MAAARCELO BIELSA! MAAARCELO BIELSA!' rang around the stadium, a statement to the board that the legendary Argentinian should never have been let go. Next, Andrea Radrizzani received his own personal message, 'THIS IS ON YOU, THIS IS ON YOOOUUU, RADRIZZANI, THIS IS ON YOU!' The fans weren't finished yet, chanting 'SACK THE BOARD!' at the directors' box, but after two minutes of mutiny it was back to supporting the players on the pitch.

There was just five minutes left, and just one goal was required to escape the relegation zone.

Football is a funny old game, and if Danny Welbeck had headed into an empty net from five yards Elland Road would have been a cauldron of hate and apathy for the final minutes of the game. Instead, Welbeck somehow headed wide, paving the way for history to be rewritten.

It was the 93rd minute, and Leeds were on the attack with Llorente in possession, 30 yards from goal with almost every player in front of him. Joe Gelhardt had still managed to find some space to the right of the box, but when he received the ball all 11 Brighton players were inside their own penalty area defending their goal. And Gelhardt took every one of them out of the game with arguably the greatest piece of skill I'd ever seen at Elland Road. Having skipped around Brighton's player of the year, Marc Cucurella, young Joffy headed for the byline and twisted and turned until England international Lewis Dunk was left sprawled on the floor. A giant defender, Dunk's frame was still a large obstacle to overcome, but Gelhardt somehow had the presence of mind, confidence and ability to scoop the ball over him, skip around him, and lift a perfect cross to the back post for Pascal Struijk to nod in the equalising goal. Elland Road exploded, and so did I.

For the first time since the crucifixion I completely let myself go, though I couldn't have controlled myself if I'd tried. Leeds had given themselves a lifeline, securing the point they needed to nudge out of the relegation zone, and I was swept away physically and emotionally during a riotous Elland Road Shuffle. After wrestling free of a headlock, I climbed up on the seats, clenched every muscle in my body as tightly as I could, and screamed at the top of my lungs for as long as I could. When I could do it no longer I climbed down and could feel my heart almost beating out of my chest; what a moment. I returned to my seat and my dad compared Joffy's magic to that of Eric Cantona against Chelsea 30 years earlier, when the Frenchman juggled the ball over the head of Paul Elliott before firing into the top corner. Rod Wallace's dribble against Spurs, Tony Yeboah's volley against Liverpool, and Cantona himself could all stand aside. In the context of the situation, Joe Gelhardt had produced something the likes of which I may never see again.

The dust settled on the goal but the noise swirling around Elland Road was still deafening, as every man, woman and child screamed for a winning goal. There were still three minutes to find it and my heart was in my mouth when Joffy's next cross cannoned off the defender's arm. Mike Dean, in the penultimate match of his career, could rarely have experienced noise like this, but a referee famed for hogging the attention turned down the chance to be Leeds United's greatest hero since Joe Gelhardt and waved play on. He was immediately swarmed by white shirts and the crowd chanted for VAR, but there was no changing the decision. My heart was in my mouth again when the final kick of the game flashed across Meslier's goal, but the net didn't bulge and the full-time whistle confirmed that Leeds had dragged themselves out of the relegation zone.

On the way home we had another match to pay attention to. Everton were playing Brentford at Goodison Park and had the chance to secure their survival with a victory. My dad dropped me at home with the Toffees 2-1 up but a man down, and by the final whistle Brentford had won 3-2, with Lampard's side reduced to nine men. Only one point separated the three relegation rivals with seven days of the season remaining and it was now mathematically certain that the battle would go to the final game, though Leeds wouldn't know until Thursday night whether they would head to Brentford with their destiny in their own hands. It promised to be the longest week of my life, but thankfully, I had a work trip to Dubai to distract me, as well as footage of Joffy's assist saved to my phone, to watch over and over again during the seven-hour flight.

Aston Villa 1 Burnley 1

It had been a draining week at a trade show, and with a 7.30am flight home it was a bind to stay out to watch Aston Villa vs Burnley, which didn't kick off until 11pm (local time). I would have to get up at 5am at the latest, and wouldn't get to bed until 1.30am at the earliest, but this was a match I couldn't miss. Nothing would be decided from this game, it was just a scene-setter for 'Survival Sunday', but I had convinced myself this was the match that decided our fate. If Villa won then Leeds would survive; if they didn't Leeds were down.

At 9.30pm I said goodbye to my work colleagues and took a seat at the Belgian bar, patiently waiting for the match to start while enjoying a massive glass of Hoegaarden. With tongue in cheek, I had wondered whether Steven Gerrard would rest players ahead of Villa's final match of the season at Manchester City, where a positive result would win the Premier League for his beloved Liverpool, and at first glance it seemed he had. Philippe Coutinho had been left on the bench along with Danny Ings, who had scored in his last four matches against Burnley and was bang in form. I was annoyed at kick-off and spitting feathers by half-time as Coutinho's replacement, Emi Buendía, had crazily given away a penalty in the final minute of the half, gifting Burnley a 1-0 lead completely against the run of play.

There was another important game going on too, and at half-time Everton were 2-0 down at home to Crystal Palace, but that genuinely meant nothing to me amid my staunch belief that Leeds's only chance of staying up was if they didn't need another point. Back at Villa Park, Buendía made amends for his silly foul by equalising early in the second half, and for the rest of the match it was Aston Villa vs Nick Pope. Burnley's keeper won the day with numerous fantastic saves that edged his team out of the relegation zone, and now even a victory at Brentford wouldn't guarantee Leeds's survival. Suddenly I was regretful of the Everton comeback I hadn't previously batted an eyelid to. Lampard's men had snatched a dramatic 3-2 victory that rendered their daunting final fixture at Arsenal inconsequential; their Premier League status was secured.

Some solace could be taken from an astonishing last-minute goal-line clearance from Tyrone Mings that prevented Burnley from winning the game and only needing a point at home to Newcastle, but in my head it was all over. Leeds would lose to Brentford and were heading back to the Championship, and Marcelo Bielsa's work at the club had all been for nothing.

Brentford 1 Leeds United 2

On the night before the final day of the season I felt like I was on death row. Frankie was out and I sat in the lounge in the dark, watching *Top of the Pops 1998* which brought childhood memories flooding back, of the time Leeds were last on the rise in the Premier League. It didn't help my mood, but it was comforting to remove myself from the present day.

On Sunday morning I moped around as if I was clinically depressed. I managed to summon enough energy to hide my misery from Alessandro but was unable to partake in any conversations with Frankie, to any meaningful degree. Frankie had now done ten years as a passive Leeds fan, so she understood my plight and handled my mood perfectly, although I was too down to give her any signs of how grateful I was. At 2pm I signed off from my family duties and got ready for the pub. I'd been invited to my brother-in-law's 'Survival Sunday' party but The Alex was the best place for me, surrounded by people feeling my pain but who I wouldn't have to talk to, although Barker joined me which was always nice.

I was well aware this would be a momentous day in the club's history, but certain it would be remembered for all the wrong reasons; the day Leeds United were relegated from the Premier League for the second time. As such, I consciously dressed in black trainers, black jeans, and my black jacket – funeral attire – however, my choice of shirt proved that deep down I was allowing myself a crumb of hope. All my 'lucky' garments had by now been contaminated by the stench of defeat, but staring at me from the wardrobe was the shirt I proposed to Frankie in, nine years earlier. It still fitted well, and if any item of clothing was going to help Leeds over the line, this was surely it.

Barker had a pint of Peroni at the ready for me on arrival in The Alex, and as we spied the best spot from which to watch the game we saw the people sat on the corner table getting up to leave. It was the same table we'd sat at on the opening day of this wretched season, but it was also the same table I sat at on the evening Huddersfield Town's victory over West Brom ended Leeds's 16-year exile from the Premier League. I took it as a good sign. Two pints later and the teams were coming out, and another good sign was seeing Leeds in their lucky lilac third kit. Granted, it wasn't as lucky as last season's maroon number (six wins), but we hadn't lost in the lilac kit, yet. Leeds also hadn't lost to a promoted team since promotion, the only team boasting such a record, collecting an improbably good 2.8 points per game. Normally I'd expect this form to start evening out, but the fact that Leeds hadn't won at Brentford since August 1950 (the day my dad could well have been conceived) surely outweighed this.

The big surprise of the day was the selection of Sam Greenwood in central midfield. It was the youngster's first senior start, in the biggest game for a generation, and if that wasn't a big enough risk, he was a forward playing out of position! Judging by how badly it had gone when Marsch had thrown Lewis Bate into the team against Chelsea, and considering we had Mateusz Klich on the bench, I was fuming. Less surprising was the news that Patrick Bamford, who had been declared fit enough for a cameo from the bench if needed, was bed-ridden with a severe bout of Covid and unavailable after all. Those devilish Football Gods were at it again.

Leeds kicked off and passed the ball back to Llorente, whose hesitation allowed Ivan Toney to block his hoof upfield and race through on goal. Llorente scampered back and managed to block the striker's effort, but it was a nightmare start that must have compounded any nerves in the Leeds camp. Thankfully it was a false alarm. The visitors quickly stamped their authority on the match, looking a proper team in a hybrid of Bielsaball and 'Marschmellowball', as my dad liked to call it. The Yorkshire Pirlo was sitting deep and dictating play, looking at his brilliant best for the first time since returning to fitness, and Raphinha and Harrison both had licence to pull wide in possession, though out of possession they would bunch together along with Rodrigo and Joe Gelhart to form a 'blanket press' that was key to Marsch's zonal philosophy, and it was working a treat.

With 20 minutes on the clock it was clear that Leeds were capable of winning, and better still, word was spreading around the pub that Newcastle had been awarded a penalty at Burnley. Before this could be confirmed, Harrison slipped Gelhardt in behind the Brentford defence and the youngster slammed the ball into the roof of the net. I jumped out of my seat and into the arms of the strangers beside me – Leeds were alive and kicking, and out of the bottom three! Alas, my celebrations were rudely interrupted by replays showing that Gelhardt's shoulder was offside, and the goal was harshly ruled out. But before I could even complain about it, confirmation came through that Newcastle had taken the lead at Turf Moor. Leeds were out of the bottom three after all!

Half-time arrived with United still in the ascendancy. They hadn't managed to score and Brentford had missed the best chances, but the visitors were playing with an assured swagger that seemed to have come from absolutely nowhere. Nevertheless, the situation couldn't be more precarious; one goal in either game would change everything.

I was clock-watching from the very start of the second half, internally celebrating every five-minute sector that passed with Leeds still above the drop zone, and just after the 55-minute landmark Brentford goalkeeper David Raya inexplicably passed the ball straight to Raphinha, then tripped the Brazilian whose twinkle toes had bamboozled him, and the referee immediately pointed to the spot. What a chance to put some daylight between staying up and going down. I was so uneasy, but Raphinha displayed nerves of steel by planting the ball calmly into the top corner after a little shimmy sent Raya diving out of the way. Our talisman sprinted to the Leeds fans in the corner and I screamed with relief, and finally started to believe.

One goal could no longer change the picture – Burnley now needed two goals to go in their favour, and if we weren't quite in dreamland we certainly were three minutes later when the Burnley game flashed up on the screen with Newcastle on the attack. It meant only one thing and I immediately screamed with delight, then celebrated deliriously with the rest of the pub when Callum Wilson tucked the ball into the Burnley net. Leeds were now firmly in the driving seat and we just needed nothing stupid to happen from here on in.

Between the 70th and 80th minutes things got really stupid. First, Burnley pulled one back through Max Cornet and once again needed just two goals to go their way. Then, having made all three substitutions, Brentford were reduced to ten men when one of their players hobbled off injured. With their next attack Sergi Canós equalised with a beautiful looping header, and having been pelted with missiles when scoring at Elland Road, Canós was so delighted that he celebrated by taking his shirt off, bringing an automatic yellow card. Then, straight from the kick-off, Canós's cynical foul as Raphinha skipped past him brought a second yellow and Brentford were down to nine men! What a stroke of luck!

It was all happening so quickly and too much for me to compute. Should I be happy with playing nine men or angry at conceding to ten? I was neither, I was just shitting myself. Leeds's safety was on a knife edge again. They had their noses above water but if they conceded they were down. And if they didn't score, one Burnley goal would relegate them too. Stick or twist, Jesse?

As Leeds calmly stroked the ball around, waiting patiently for an opening, I was screaming at the telly, willing them to 'fucking go for it!' They didn't necessarily need to score, but against nine men I wanted to throw the kitchen sink at it in case Burnley did, and heading into five minutes of injury time a few long-range shots were the closest Leeds had come to scoring. With no further goals at Turf Moor the Whites were still in the box seat, but wholly reliant on not hearing any earth-shattering news from Burnley. The tension was far too great for any chanting to break out; instead the stadium was filled with an eerie hush, and when the camera panned to the away end I could see my pain etched on the faces of every Leeds fan. If they weren't biting their nails they had their hands on their heads, or their heads in their gadgets checking for

Burnley updates. One bloke even had a good old-fashioned wireless radio held to his ear.

As we entered the final minute of the season everything was still on the line, but United had a corner and I held my breath, desperate for the goal that would end this topsy-turvy relegation battle once and for all. In line with the laws of physics, a vital Leeds corner failed to beat the first man, but the clearance only bobbled to the edge of the box, where Jack Harrison was steaming towards the ball and thumped it first time towards goal. A kind deflection helped beat the dive of David Raya, and when the ball hit the back of the net all the pain and suffering of the past few weeks and months was instantly extinguished. Leeds had done it, they were safe, and the pub transcended into ecstasy!

By the time I'd regained any sense of composure the final whistle had gone in both matches, and the jubilant players flocked to the corner of the Brentford Community Stadium where 1,700 Leeds fans were housed. A wonderful party ensued, and although I wished I could have been present, it was almost as joyous just watching the scenes. Raphinha hopped into the away end and made his way up to the top section to embrace his girlfriend in the manner of a Wimbledon champion, and there he remained, jumping up and down with the supporters and waving a Brazil flag as his team-mates lined up in front of them all, everyone singing and bouncing along, 'WE ALL LOVE LEEDS, WE ALL LOVE LEEDS, WE ALL LOVE LEEDS, WE ALL LOVE LEEDS!' What a sight to behold, euphoric scenes the likes of which I'd only witnessed twice in 30 years supporting the club, and the tears that had filled my eyes began to roll down my face. What an afternoon, what a season!

On the triumphant walk home from The Alex I rang Lewis in Canada, just as I had done after the defeat at Brentford that ended our automatic promotion push in Bielsa's first season. Back in 2019 we were distraught as we dissected what had gone wrong, but this time we revelled in the glory of our miraculous escape: the last-minute goals against Norwich and Brighton, the improbable turnaround against Wolves, and the crazy circumstances that had unfolded at Brentford. We concluded that the Football Gods had finally pulled through for us, offering redemption for the behind-closed-doors era that stole the best period of our Leeds-supporting lives, and for the chain of events that stole The Great Man from us.

I spent the evening on Twitter, a great place to be at a time like this, which was elevated by the news that Leeds's escape had triggered a pre-agreed deal to sign US international midfielder Brenden Aaronson from Red Bull Salzburg for £25m. Coupled with this was the realisation that Raphinha's relegation release clause (set ludicrously low at £21m) could not be activated, and the following morning reports emerged that Leeds had rejected a £50m bid from Barcelona for the Brazilian. I'd never loved the Premier League more! Just 24 hours earlier I'd been trying to justify life in the Championship, now I couldn't be more elated to have avoided it.

And I truly was elated. The misery I'd felt ever since El Loco was sacked had disappeared, a misery that had leaked into normal life and led me to believe other factors were to blame for my low moods. Lack of sleep, stress of work, strains of fatherhood; it was none of those, it was just being a Leeds fan! With our Premier League status confirmed I felt myself again, and I was finally ready to move into stage five of my grief, acceptance.

Premier League table 2021/22

	Pld	W	D	L	F	A	Pts
Manchester City	38	29	6	3	99	26	93
Liverpool	38	28	8	2	94	26	92
Chelsea	38	21	11	6	76	33	74
Tottenham Hotspur	38	22	5	11	69	40	71
Arsenal	38	22	3	13	61	48	69
Manchester United	38	16	10	12	57	57	58
West Ham United	38	16	8	14	60	51	56
Leicester City	38	14	10	14	62	59	52
Brighton & Hove Albion	38	12	15	11	42	44	51
Wolverhampton Wanderers	38	15	6	17	38	43	51
Newcastle United	38	13	10	15	44	62	49
Crystal Palace	38	11	15	12	50	46	48
Brentford	38	13	7	18	48	56	46
Aston Villa	38	13	6	19	52	54	45
Southampton	38	9	13	16	43	67	40
Everton	38	11	6	21	43	66	39
LEEDS UNITED	**38**	**9**	**11**	**18**	**42**	**79**	**38**
Burnley	38	7	14	17	34	53	35
Watford	38	6	5	27	34	77	23
Norwich City	38	5	7	26	23	84	22

Epilogue

LEEDS UNITED'S history has been significantly enriched by the four seasons of Marcelo Bielsa. The Great Man created a team that embodied everything the Leeds fans wish to see, with commitment levels beyond anything we could have demanded as the players dedicated their lives to becoming the fittest team since sports bras made the metric measurable. They played in the image of their leader, with honesty and integrity, and while future generations will be told about their vibrant, fearless, high-intensity football, only those lucky few who witnessed it in the flesh could ever feel the emotion of it: the passion, the aggression, the determination. Bielsaball at full throttle was like nothing else, and his tenure will never be forgotten.

The board ripped up his blueprint and were starting again, but they were doing so in the Premier League because of Marcelo, and you can be sure future Leeds United owners will appoint managers with the intention of returning to El Loco's unique brand of scintillating football. And so the dream lives on, that Marcelo Bielsa's influence will one day deliver Leeds to the real promised land of European champions, and that the football world will one day bow to the old adage, 'In the Loco Way, one lives better,' because if they did, our sport truly would be the Beautiful Game.

First Impressions of Bielsaball

Liverpool manager Jürgen Klopp, September 2020: 'Leeds are special. They performed outstandingly and it was very difficult. For 95 minutes, by the way!'

Fulham manager Scott Parker, September 2020: 'A tough side, we all know that. Every team, every manager, every player that goes up against a Leeds team fully understand what they're up against.'

Sheffield United manager Chris Wilder, September 2020: 'Bielsa is an outstanding figure in European and world football.'

Manchester City manager Pep Guardiola, October 2020: 'Leeds had their moments because they are an incredible team, a fantastic team.'

Wolverhampton Wanderers manager Nuno Espírito Santo, October 2020: 'The dynamic of Leeds was amazing. They have balance, they have breakers, they create chances, and we needed to be humble enough to recognise that.'

Aston Villa manager Dean Smith, October 2020: 'They were very good. We probably got away with a 0-3 in the end with the chances they had.'

Leicester City manager Brendan Rodgers, November 2020: 'It's the type of performance you need to beat a team like Leeds. They have shown what a really good attacking team they are.'

Crystal Palace winger Andros Townsend, November 2020: 'When you watch on TV you don't get the full view of the way they play. They're incredible, very special. It was great to experience it in the flesh.'

Arsenal manager Mikel Arteta, November 2020: 'They always go full gas. They are very loyal to their principles and approach every game in the same way, which is to be very aggressive with and without the ball and try to win.'

Everton manager Carlo Ancelotti, November 2020: 'They played really well. They have a clear idea of football, create a lot of problems for teams they play against. It's a really, really good team.'

Chelsea striker Olivier Giroud, December 2020: 'One of the best teams I have faced this season. Physically they run everywhere, it was so hard. They really impress me.'

West Ham United manager David Moyes, December 2020: 'This game is different to any other you play in the Premier League, Leeds have got something different.'

Newcastle United manager Steve Bruce, December 2020: 'He [Marcelo Bielsa] transformed Leeds. I've never seen anyone have an impact like it with the same players. He's right at the top.'

Manchester United manager Ole Gunnar Solskjær, December 2020: 'They play the same way whether they're 4-0 up, 4-0 down, or it's 0-0. They do that every game. We said at half-time that it's not going to stop, you have to run until the final whistle goes.'

Burnley manager Sean Dyche, December 2020: 'I'm not bothered about what they do. They've had an up and down season so far.'

West Bromwich Albion manager Sam Allardyce, December 2020: 'Leeds ended up with a 5-0 win and deservedly so.'

Tottenham Hotspur striker Son Heung-min, January 2021: 'It was a really difficult game. They are doing an unbelievable job and they work so hard.'

Brighton & Hove Albion manager Graham Potter, January 2021: 'I think he [Bielsa] has done a fantastic job and everyone at Leeds United has done really well.'

Bielsa Era Stats

Team

	Pld	W	D	L	F	A	PPG	Win%
All competitions	170	80	33	57	256	219	N/A	47%
Full league record	158	77	30	51	244	203	1.65	49%
Premier League record	64	23	13	28	91	114	1.28	36%
PL with Kalvin Phillips	40	18	11	11	62	51	1.63	45%
PL without Kalvin Phillips	24	5	2	17	29	63	0.71	21%

Players
(League appearances only)

Goalkeepers	Apps	Conceded	Assists	Average rating
Illan Meslier	71	115	0	7.23
Kiko Casilla	58	57	0	6.71
Bailey Peacock-Farrell	28	32	0	6.89

Defenders	Apps	Goals	Assists	Average rating
Luke Ayling	132	8	15	7.26
Ezgjan Alioski	119	15	12	6.75
Liam Cooper	115	6	2	7.29
Pascal Struijk	50	1	0	7.02

Ben White	46	1	1	7.61
Barry Douglas	42	0	6	6.83
Gaetano Berradi	39	0	1	7.15
Pontus Jansson	39	3	1	7.41
Diego Llorente	34	3	0	7.21
Robin Koch	26	0	0	7.19
Junior Firpo	24	0	2	6.50

Midfielders	Apps	Goals	Assists	Average rating
Mateusz Klich	149	21	22	6.85
Stuart Dallas	134	18	7	7.04
Kalvin Phillips	121	4	6	7.67
Pablo Hernández	93	21	26	7.22
Adam Forshaw	52	0	1	6.87
Samuel Sáiz	19	0	1	6.79

Wingers	Apps	Goals	Assists	Average rating
Jack Harrison	144	22	25	6.88
Hélder Costa	66	7	9	6.67
Raphinha	54	17	12	7.06
Dan James	32	4	2	6.38
Jack Clarke	25	2	2	6.68
Ian Poveda	18	0	0	6.56

Strikers	Apps	Goals	Assists	Average rating
Patrick Bamford	112	44	15	6.67
Tyler Roberts	100	9	9	6.71
Rodrigo Moreno	45	13	4	6.87
Kemar Roofe	32	15	1	6.72

Joe Gelhardt	17	1	1	7.00
Eddie Nketiah	14	3	1	6.79

Extras	Apps	Goals	Assists	Average rating
Leif Davis	10	0	0	6.30
Lewis Baker	9	0	0	5.67
Jordan Stevens	5	0	0	5.80
Aapo Halme	3	0	0	7.00
Crysencio Summerville	3	0	0	6.33
Cody Drameh	3	0	0	5.67
Tom Pearce	2	0	0	6.00
Oliver Casey	2	0	0	6.00
Izzy Brown	2	0	0	5.00
Charlie Cresswell	2	0	0	7.00
Leo Hjelde	2	0	0	7.00
Will Huffer	1	0	0	7.00
Ryan Edmondson	1	0	0	6.00
Robbie Gotts	1	0	0	6.00
Mateusz Bogusz	1	0	0	6.00
Sam Greenwood	1	0	0	6.00
Lewis Bate	1	0	0	7.00
Stuart McKinstry	1	0	0	6.00
Liam McCarron	1	0	0	6.00
Niall Huggins	1	0	0	6.00